An Atlas

of

HARROGATE

by

J. A. PATMORE

B. Litt., M.A.

Maps drawn by

A. G. HODGKISS

P. JOAN TREASURE

J. LYNCH

THE CORPORATION OF HARROGATE

1963

Contents

		Page
Preface by J. Neville Knox, Town Clerk of Harrogate		v
Introduction		1
1.	The development of British spas	3
2.	Setting	7
3.	Site	9
4.	Origins	13
5.	Georgian and Regency villages	15
6.	The mid-nineteenth Century	19
7.	The Threshold of Change	21
8.	The Advent of the Railway	23
9.	Victorian Spa	25
10.	The changing Town Centre	27
11.	Residential Expansion	29
12.	Visitors	31
13.	The changing Resort	35
14.	The contemporary Spa	37
15.	The Season	39
16.	Shopping and other Services	41
17.	Administration and Industry	43
18.	The movement of Labour	47
19.	Municipal Services and Local Government	49
	Financial and Housing Data	50
	Climatic Data	51
	Bibliography	52

List of Illustrations

Plate			Facing page
I	(a)	THE SUN PAVILION, VALLEY GARDENS	vi
	(b)	THE ROYAL PUMP ROOM MUSEUM AND ROYAL PARADE	
II	(a)	THE OLD SULPHUR WELL IN 1773	1
	(b)	THE OLD SULPHUR WELL IN 1829	
	(c)	THE OLD SULPHUR WELL IN 1880	
	(d)	THE ROYAL PUMP ROOM MUSEUM TODAY	
III	(a)	HIGH HARROGATE IN 1831	1
	(b)	LOW HARROGATE IN 1829	
IV		AN AERIAL VIEW OF THE TOWN CENTRE	1
V	(a)	THE MONTPELLIER BATHS	16
	(b)	THE SPA ROOMS	
VI	(a)	THE CRIMPLE VIADUCT IN 1847	17
	(b)	THE RAILWAY IN CENTRAL HARROGATE *circa* 1862	
VII	(a)	PROSPECT HILL *circa* 1890	32
	(b)	THE VALLEY GARDENS *circa* 1900	
VIII	(a)	PARLIAMENT STREET *circa* 1890	33
	(b)	JAMES STREET *circa* 1900	
IX		THE SPA AREA OF LOW HARROGATE	44
X		THE COMMERCIAL AREA OF CENTRAL HARROGATE	45
XI	(a)	THE HEADQUARTERS OF THE LEEDS REGIONAL HOSPITAL BOARD	48
	(b)	STRAY TOWERS AND STRAYSIDE COURT	
	(c)	BERKELEY HOUSE	
	(d)	ROBERT HIRST & CO. LTD.	
XII	(a)	DUNLOPILLO DIVISION, DUNLOP RUBBER CO. LTD.	49
	(b)	FIBRES DIVISION HEADQUARTERS, IMPERIAL CHEMICAL INDUSTRIES LTD.	
	(c)	MULTI-STOREY FLAT DEVELOPMENT, PARK PLACE	
	(d)	CENTRAL AREA REDEVELOPMENT, PARLIAMENT STREET	

Preface

J. Neville Knox
(Town Clerk of Harrogate)

I KNOW the town will be extremely grateful to Mr. J. A. Patmore for his up-to-date record of the growth of Harrogate. Harrogate's heyday as a spa was in the late Victorian and early Edwardian eras and there is no doubt that it was fast running down between the two World War periods. I think it can be said that Harrogate is one of the few places to which the 1939-45 War was a blessing in disguise. Whereas prior to that all the eggs were in the 'spa' basket, the town's economy is now based on five principal foundations and has never been sounder than it is today.

Firstly, it remains a very attractive residential town, not only for those who work within its borders but for many who work in the industrial West Riding and for those who are not necessarily tied to any specific town, such as representatives covering the north of England as well as those who retire here.

Secondly, it is a shopping centre for a very wide area with many branches of London shops and people come to shop in Harrogate from as far away as Tyneside and the other side of the Pennines besides most Yorkshire towns.

Thirdly, it has become an important administrative centre with the advent of such firms as Imperial Chemical Industries (Fibres Division), Messrs. Cawood Whartons, Messrs. Dunlop Rubber Co. Ltd. (Dunlopillo Division), Mercantile Credit Co. Ltd., Associated Chemical Companies, etc.

Fourthly, it is still a spa and holiday resort with as many treatments being done, in conjunction with the Leeds Regional Hospital Board, as during its heyday as a spa.

Fifthly, it has an extensive conference and trade fair business which is the backbone of the hotel industry.

In all this the local authority has been able to play a vital part and has helped to fashion, both directly and indirectly, the present prosperous pattern, whilst maintaining the town's character and amenities. It is the Council's policy that this pattern should continue. Private house building is encouraged and continues at a high level, the latest projects including the building of multi-storey flats. Important additions are being made to the shopping centre through enlightened planning. New administrative centres are actively encouraged to come to the town and the maximum facilities are provided to extend the spa, conference and trade fair business. The present decade will consolidate and even advance on that which has taken place in the last.

This could well entail a revision of part of Mr. Patmore's book in future editions so that the Atlas is always up to date. The Atlas is a notable contribution to both the history and present life of the town and will, I am sure, be avidly consulted by a great variety of people both in and out of its borders. I am convinced that it will be a most successful publication and I sincerely congratulate Mr. Patmore on it.

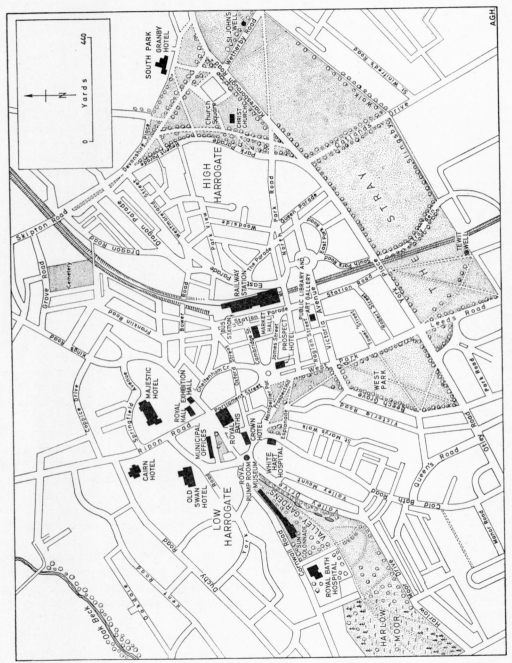

The central area today.

Plate I. The Resort Today

(*a*) The Sun Pavilion, Valley Gardens.   *Photograph: Bertram Unné*

(*b*) The entrance to the Valley Gardens, with the Royal Pump Room Museum and Royal Parade beyond.   *Photograph: Bertram Unné*

Plate II. The Old Sulphur Well (now the Royal Pump Room Museum)

(b) In 1829. A lithograph by Day and Haghe from a drawing by James Stubbs. The cover over the well was erected in 1804, and was transferred to the Tewit Well in 1842.

(d) In 1962, with the Annexe erected in 1913.

Photograph: Bertram Unné

(a) In 1773, from a drawing by Moses Griffith. The area is still almost completely open, with only rudimentary covers over the springs.

Reproduction by gracious permission of H.R.H. the Princess Royal

(c) In 1880, from an early photograph. The cover was built in 1842, and this photograph shows the original dolphin finial.

Plate III. The Regency Villages

(a) High Harrogate in 1831. Lithographed by C. Hullmandel from a drawing by John Field. The newly erected Christ Church is seen to the right, and the original St. John's Well in the centre. The view emphasizes the open nature of the village, and the use of the Stray as a promenade.

(b) Low Harrogate in 1829 from the top of Prospect Hill. Lithographed by C. Hullmandel from a drawing by James Stubbs. The almost completely rural setting of this part of the spa is striking.

Plate IV

An aerial view of the town centre, looking north-east. The Royal Pump Room Museum is in the centre foreground, the Municipal Offices and the Royal Hall in the middle distance on the left, and the railway station in the right background.
Photograph: Aerofilms Ltd.

Introduction

HARROGATE holds a peculiar fascination for me. This fascination is not only that of an extremely pleasant resort, or even that of the place in which I received much of my schooling, but it stems from the very nature of the town itself. In the first instance, there is the prospect of a town virtually created to satisfy the short-lived demands of Victorian and Edwardian society, and then having to recognize that as a spa, or even as an inland resort alone, it was increasingly an anachronism. It is even more stimulating to observe its growing success in the adaptation of its way of life, and its coming to make a very necessary contribution to the economic and social functioning of the wider area in which it is set.

It was only regrettable that such a unique town had no adequate recent account of the development of its landscape and its functions. W. Grainge's history was published in 1871, when Harrogate had only 6775 inhabitants. Of more recent works, W. Haythornthwaite's *Harrogate Story* (1954) was largely concerned with the social history of Harrogate prior to its incorporation as a Borough in 1884, and H. H. Walker's *Harrogate's Past* (1959) with the history of its local government.

It was therefore timely when the Publicity Committee and the Library and Arts Committee decided to sponsor jointly a new account of the town. I was asked to write for them, and it was decided that an atlas format would be the most useful form of presentation. I am most grateful to these Committees, and to the Council who endorsed their decision, for this opportunity. It must, however, be made clear in fairness to them that I alone am responsible for the conclusions I have drawn, and for the manner in which I have expressed them.

Far too many people have assisted me to make individual mention possible, and I trust I may be forgiven for not listing them all by name. I should have been helpless without their ready assistance, and to them all I offer my warm thanks. I would, however, make particular mention of those officials of Harrogate Corporation who have given me so much of their time and listened patiently to my requests. The enthusiasm of the Town Clerk, Mr. J. Neville Knox, did much to launch the Atlas, the Borough Librarian, Mr. J. Stuffins, has acted as liaison with the Council, and, together with his assistants in the Reference Library, has placed his wide knowledge of sources at my disposal. The Publicity and Entertainments Manager, Mr. W. W. Baxter, and his assistants at the Information Bureau and the Royal Baths, gave me a real insight into the basic functions of the town. These three officers also read the manuscript and made many helpful comments and corrections.

Any atlas is only as good as its maps, and I have been singularly fortunate in having at my disposal the skill and interest of the cartographic staff of the Department of Geography, the University of Liverpool, Mr. A. G. Hodgkiss, Miss P. J. Treasure and Mr. J. Lynch. I am grateful too for the stimulus and help freely given by my colleagues in the University of Liverpool, particularly Professor R. W. Steel who has liberally made available facilities for me to undertake this work. A final word of thanks is due to Professor E. W. Gilbert, Professor of Geography in the University of Oxford, who supervised the original research on which this Atlas is based and whose scholarly care has had a great influence on my work.

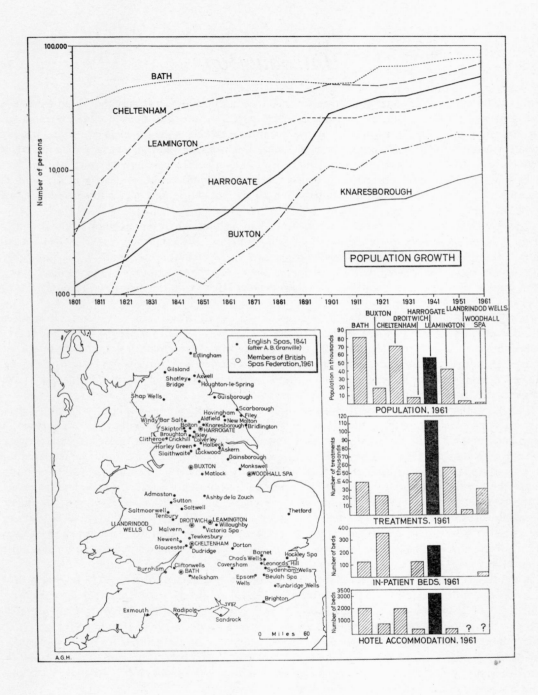

POPULATION GROWTH

Number of persons

100,000

BATH

CHELTENHAM

LEAMINGTON

HARROGATE

KNARESBOROUGH

BUXTON

10,000

1000

1801 1811 1821 1831 1841 1851 1861 1871 1881 1891 1901 1911 1921 1931 1941 1951 1961

● English Spas, 1841
(after A. B. Granville)

○ Members of British
Spas Federation, 1961

Edlingham

Gilsland

Shotley
Bridge

Axwell

Houghton-le-Spring

Shap Wells

Guisborough

Scarborough

Hovingham

Filey

Windy Bar Salt

Aldfield

New Malton

Bolton

Knaresborough

Bridlington

Skipton

HARROGATE

Broughton

Ilkley

Clitheroe

Crickhill

Calverley

Holbeck

Harley Green

Lockwood

Askern

Slaithwaite

Gainsborough

BUXTON

Monkswell

Matlock

WOODHALL SPA

Admaston

Ashby de la Zouch

Sutton

Saltwell

Saltmoorwell

Thetford

Tenbury

DROITWICH

LEAMINGTON

LLANDRINDOD
WELLS

Willoughby

Malvern

Victoria Spa

Newent

Tewkesbury

Gloucester

CHELTENHAM

Dorton

Dudridge

Barnet

Chad's Wells

Hockley Spa

Cliftonwells

Caversham

Leonards Hill

Burnham

BATH

Sydenham Wells

Melksham

Epsom
Wells

Beulah Spa

Tunbridge Wells

Brighton

Exmouth

Radipole

Sandrock

0   Miles   60

A.G.H.

BATH   BUXTON   DROITWICH   HARROGATE   LLANDRINDOD WELLS
CHELTENHAM   LEAMINGTON   WOODHALL SPA

Population in thousands

90
80
70
60
50
40
30
20
10

POPULATION, 1961

Number of treatments
in thousands

120
110
100
90
80
70
60
50
40
30
20
10

TREATMENTS. 1961

Number of beds

400

300

200

100

IN-PATIENT BEDS, 1961

Number of beds

3500
3000
2000
1000

?   ?

HOTEL ACCOMMODATION. 1961

2

1 The development of British spas

BRITISH spas have had a colourful if often chequered history. Today there remain only seven active spas in England and Wales, but in 1841 Dr. Granville showed seventy on his map of 'the principal mineral springs' of England and in the early eighteenth century Thomas Short noticed 228 'spaws', 'besides several others of less note'.

By 'spaws', Short was referring only to the springs themselves and not to any associated villages or towns. A careful distinction must in fact be drawn between the medical and social creation which is the spa itself, and the settlement to which it may give rise. In their eighteenth-century heyday, the spas were close-knit communities, where all activities centred on the taking of the waters and the exclusive social round which accompanied it. Their later increase in size contained the seeds of the decay of their traditional way of life, such changes, in Granville's words, 'converting a spa with a town into a town with a spa — a state of things seldom favourable to the duration of the latter'. Today, most of the spa towns are indeed towns with a spa rather than the reverse. They range in size from Bath, with 80,856 inhabitants in 1961, to Woodhall Spa with 1990. The extent of their medical facilities as spas, however, bears little relation to the size of their population, as the diagram shows. Woodhall lags only a little behind Bath in the number of treatments given at spa establishments. The second largest town, Cheltenham, now has no facilities for treatment, whilst Harrogate, averaging 120,000 treatments annually, far outstrips its nearest rival, Leamington. There is even more variation in the facilities available for in-patients at specialized spa hospitals. Three spas have no facilities, whilst Harrogate has 249 beds and Buxton 350. Such contrasts, and the relation of spa activity to the size of the town, are indications of the extent to which the spa function has ceased to be dominant in many of the towns. The 'spas' have rather become in varying degree inland resorts, shopping, service and administrative centres, residential and industrial towns.

Nevertheless, it was as spas that most of them grew to importance. The term *spa* itself was first applied in English to Harrogate. Its derivation is the Walloon *espa*, a fountain, and was coined from Spa, the Belgian town sixteen miles south-west of Liège, where the use of the waters for curative purposes dates back to 1326. Edmund Deane, in his *Spadacrene Anglica* of 1626, attributes the use of the word to Timothy Bright, who gave the name *the English Spaw* to the Tewit Well at Harrogate about 1596.

The origins of the modern British spa date from the late sixteenth century. The thermal waters of Bath (and perhaps those of Buxton too) were used for bathing in Roman times, but the essentially rural society of early medieval England had little use for such a resort. In the later Middle Ages many flocked in pilgrimage to springs or holy wells which were credited with magical cures, but there was little concept of any inherent worth in the waters themselves. After the Renaissance came renewed impetus, when the medical profession began to place trust in the therapeutic value of mineral waters, and publicized the virtues of the cure in their writings. In the seventeenth century, this flow of literature became prolific and promoted the interests of several spas prior to the Civil War.

The expansion of activity was not fortuitous. The increased medical interest of the Renaissance gave the initial impetus, but the increased prosperity of England in late Tudor times gave rise to a leisured class with money and time to spare, and increased commerce brought an increase in travelling for both business and pleasure. Hitherto London and the larger provincial towns had been the only resorts in any sense of the term, and the new spas provided an additional outlet.

They were still, however, primarily medical in purpose, often with little accommodation and few formal facilities for taking the waters. As such, they survived the Puritan regime relatively unscathed. With the Restoration, conditions changed rapidly in their favour. Conscious seeking after pleasure by the wealthy and leisured upper class stimulated the social development of the spa, whilst the spirit of scientific enquiry, symbolized by the establishment of the Royal Society in 1662, brought a new critical and analytical approach to medical treatment.

These trends were accentuated in the eighteenth century, aptly termed by R. B. Mowat 'an age of watering places'. Medically, much treatment was on almost modern lines, and the work of such spa doctors as Oliver at Bath was justly famous. But their real importance was social rather than medical. As Defoe observed in 1724, 'the coming to the Wells to drink the waters was a mere Matter of Custom; some drink, more do not, and few drink physically. But Company and Diversion is, in short, the main business of the Place'. As centres of social life, the spas had no rivals outside London, but it was a life of ordered formality, social organization being carried to the very smallest detail. The arbiter of spa fashion was Bath, and at the beginning of the eighteenth century Bath, and its Master of Ceremonies, Beau Nash, were almost synonymous. The pattern of living required a formal range of equipment: the baths and pump rooms were accompanied by assembly rooms, parades, libraries and theatres in a distinctive landscape.

The very success of the spas contained the seeds of their decay. They could not maintain their exclusive way of life as they became larger: inevitably they became more truly resorts, and, after 1750, suffered further through the rise of their coastal counterparts. Their importance was maintained during the Napoleonic Wars, when access to continental spas was prohibited, and the rise of new spas such as Cheltenham and Leamington added vigour. Nevertheless, their's was now a genteel role: the Bath of Jane Austen contrasted strongly with that of Nash. The majority remained little more than large villages. Bath alone was a substantial town, with 33,196 inhabitants in 1801, but was no longer expanding rapidly.

Renewed impetus came in the second half of the nineteenth century, and in some ways the spas reverted to the first period of their existence as once more the pursuit of health became paramount. There, however, similarity ended. The new health resorts now had a fully urban form and were consequently far fewer in number. Medically, too, there were many changes. The empirical 'Cure' was still taken by many visitors as an accepted part of the social round, but there was an increasingly scientific basis of practice. The scope of treatment was gradually broadened, and the spas acquired an important reputation for the relief or cure of rheumatism and allied disorders.

In addition to the rebirth of established spas, new spas such as Woodhall and Llandrindod Wells came into being. They were often little more than villages in size, but had a range of facilities far in excess of the eighteenth-century spas. The hydropathic movement also had its adherents. At Matlock it was instrumental in reviving a decayed spa, and through it the pure waters of Malvern and Ben Rhydding became the effective basis of health resorts.

The zenith of the Victorian spa was reached by 1914. The social levelling of the years following the First World War reduced the demand for the socially significant Cure. As towns, the spas began slowly, but inevitably, to change, seeking new bases for a continued urban existence. The establishment of the National Health Service in 1948 brought a great increase of business to the spas, but the new clientele does not bring revenue to the hoteliers in the manner of their predecessors of Edwardian days. Medically, the range of treatments available continued to increase, whilst the empirical drinking Cure virtually ceased to exist. Today, the spas are essentially centres for physical treatment in the broadest sense of the term, using methods of hydrotherapy, massage, remedial gymnastics and electrotherapy. Their role is clearly recognized, though not always accepted, by the medical profession, for, in the words of the B.M.A.'s booklet, *The Spa in Medical Practice* (1951), 'the future of British spas will depend not so much upon the presence of natural medicinal waters, or their specific therapeutic value, as upon a proper orientation of all modern methods of treatment integrated into the natural and developed amenities provided by the spa locality'.

Against this general picture of the development of the spa concept, the growth of individual spa towns must be considered. Each successive phase in the medical and social history of spas has been characterized by the ascendancy of particular spas. In terms of size alone, this is illustrated by the graph of the growth of the population of the five largest spa towns. The graph is constructed in such a way that the same rate of growth, whatever the size of the town, is represented by a line of the same inclination. It clearly shows the initial pre-eminence of Bath, and its subsequent failure to recapture the vigour of its Georgian heyday, the Regency expansion of Cheltenham and Leamington, and the Victorian revival of Buxton and Harrogate.

These variations in growth are the product of the unique circumstances of each spa, and of the stimuli responsible for its development. Many spas remained obscure for long periods before their waters were effectively exploited, and many indeed were destined for obscurity. The stimuli leading to exploitation varied widely in nature and effect, and their application in a particular instance was often fortuitous. The initial discovery of the therapeutic properties of a spring was usually accidental, and its further reputation then depended on medical approval and fashionable favour. These alone were insufficient to ensure continued growth: close proximity or easy access to major centres of population was a considerable advantage, but with the increasing sophistication of spa life and treatment, the conscious private or municipal provision of facilities for taking the waters was of prime importance.

It is the purpose of this atlas to examine the particular case of Harrogate, to consider the stimuli which occasioned its genesis and evolution as a spa, and its subsequent progress as a town when its possession of a spa was no longer alone sufficient to sustain its urban form.

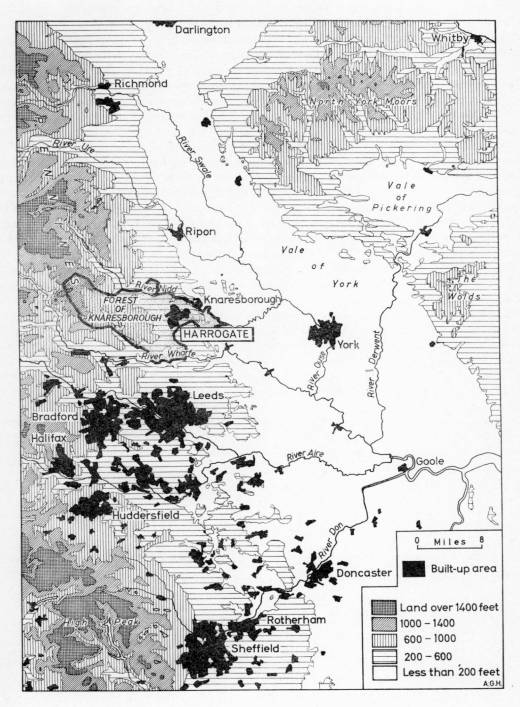

Darlington

Richmond

River Ure

River Swale

North York Moors

Whitby

Ripon

Vale of Pickering

River Nidd

FOREST OF KNARESBOROUGH

Knaresborough

HARROGATE

River Wharfe

Vale of York

The Wolds

York

Bradford

Leeds

Halifax

River Ouse

River Derwent

Huddersfield

River Aire

Goole

River Don

Doncaster

High Peak

Rotherham

Sheffield

0 Miles 8

■ Built-up area

Land over 1400 feet

1000 – 1400

600 – 1000

200 – 600

Less than 200 feet

A.G.H.

2 Setting

THE facts of Harrogate's position are simple, but they have had a marked effect on its growth. It lies in the marginal tract between the western edge of the Vale of York and the eastern flanks of the central Pennines, 15 miles to the north of Leeds and the industrial West Riding, and 20 miles to the west of York.

Some 3 miles to the east lies the market town of Knaresborough, occupying the same general position, but with a vastly different and much longer history. It is built on the eastern bank of the Nidd where that river has carved a gorge 100 ft. deep, a site with an obvious potential for defence. The defensive value of this site led to the choice of Knaresborough in the early twelfth century as the military stronghold from which control over the newly established Royal hunting Forest of Knaresborough could be exercised. The Forest stretched away towards the higher moorland of the west, and included within it was the site of what would eventually become Harrogate.

As the military importance of Knaresborough faded, its commercial significance increased. It was situated in a zone of general north–south movement (although no main north–south roads now pass through it), and, even more important, it lay at the junction of contrasting agricultural areas. It is one of a series of market towns which lie at the exit of the main valleys of the Pennines into the Vale of York. They command routeways into and across the Pennines, and lie in a zone of interchange of contrasting agricultural products.

In the nineteenth century Harrogate outstripped Knaresborough in size, and by nature of its size usurped many of the latter's functions, for it occupied a comparable position. Its initial siting was occasioned by the location of its springs, but its development was made easier by its position. It was in close proximity to, and within easy access of potential sources of visitors — the landed gentry of the Vale, and the industrial *nouveaux riches* of the West Riding. The relief of the area was sufficiently subdued to enable new lines of communication to be created without major difficulty when demand justified it: both the main road and rail routes from Leeds to the north now pass through Harrogate.

In more recent times, this position has given additional advantages. It is on the threshold of the scenic attractions of the Yorkshire Dales, and within easy reach of the contrasted landscapes of the North Riding. Even in Georgian times, the wide range of possible excursions was a major attraction to the spa, despite much severer limits on travel. The ruins of Bolton Abbey, to the west in Wharfedale, were about as far as the visitor would normally go. It was then an expensive and fatiguing excursion. A diarist of 1816 recorded that a coach and four for such a visit cost £3 3s. 9d. and ''tis almost too much to do, in one day, for pleasure'.

Today, Harrogate is sufficiently close to the industrial areas to the south to make it a convenient dormitory for them. In a wider context, its position approximately midway between London and Edinburgh has made it an important overnight stopping place for travellers between north and south.

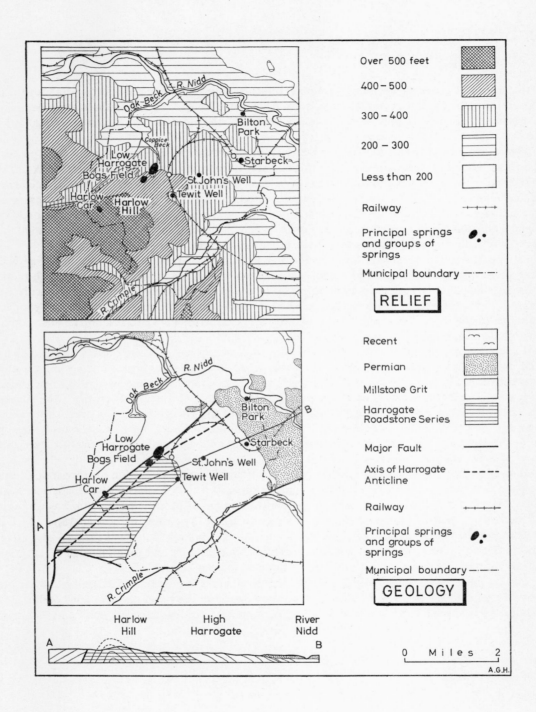

Over 500 feet
400 – 500
300 – 400
200 – 300
Less than 200
Railway
Principal springs
and groups of
springs
Municipal boundary

RELIEF

Recent
Permian
Millstone Grit
Harrogate
Roadstone Series
Major Fault
Axis of Harrogate
Anticline
Railway
Principal springs
and groups of
springs
Municipal boundary

GEOLOGY

R. Nidd
Oak Beck
Coppice Beck
Bilton Park
Starbeck
Low Harrogate Bogs Field
St. John's Well
Tewit Well
Harlow Car
Harlow Hill
R. Crimple

Oak Beck
R. Nidd
Bilton Park
B
Starbeck
Low Harrogate Bogs Field
St. John's Well
Tewit Well
Harlow Car
A
R. Crimple

Harlow Hill   High Harrogate   River Nidd
A   B

0   Miles   2

A.G.H.

8

3 Site

THE sites of few towns have been more arbitrarily determined than those of the spas. In this Harrogate is no exception. The origin and distribution of its mineral springs will be considered later, but because it was built around them the town now lies in a peculiarly elevated position, athwart the ridge separating the valleys of the Oak Beck and the Crimple. The ridge itself is relatively flat, though rising gently south-west to a height of 600 ft. on Harlow Hill. Almost the whole of the town is built on land over 350 ft. high, the only considerable depression below this level being the valley of Coppice Beck, which drains the spa area of Low Harrogate. To the north-west, the Oak Beck flows in a rather deep, narrow valley, which formed part of an overflow system from the Washburn valley to the west in glacial times. In contrast, the Crimple valley is broad and open, the river meandering gently across its floor. The continuous built-up area of the town has grown to the rim of both valleys, but as yet has penetrated neither.

The moderate relief masks a geological structure of some complexity, which is responsible for the occurrence of the springs. Harrogate is sited just to the west of the outcrops of rocks of Permian age (of which the yellowish Magnesian Limestone gives a characteristic colour to the buildings of Knaresborough), and lies almost entirely on rocks of the Carboniferous period. Of these the coarse pebbly sandstone of the Millstone Grit is dominant. It was used extensively in the building of Harrogate; there are several local quarries though none are now actively exploited. The Grit weathers to a very dark colour, and, coupled with slate as the dominant roofing material, gives a sombre appearance to the centre of the town. To the west of Harrogate, the ground continues to rise, and open moorland developed on the acid soils of the Millstone Grit is reached within 3 miles of the town centre, at a height of about 700 ft.

The Carboniferous rocks are folded along a north-east–south-west axis, and this structure exposes older rocks, the Harrogate Roadstone series of inter-bedded sandstones and shales, at its core. The upfold, known as the Harrogate Anticline, is assymetrical in section, the northern limb dipping more steeply, the beds being inclined up to 80° from the horizontal. The structure is further complicated by a series of faults, of which the most important lies only a short distance north-west of the axis of the upfold, and runs parallel to it.

This structure has influenced the distribution of Harrogate's mineral springs on which its reputation as a spa was founded. The springs are characterized by both their number and their variety. Eighty-eight are known within a radius of 2 miles of the town centre, though only sixteen are used medicinally. They fall into two main groups, sulphur waters and chalybeate waters, though they can be further subdivided according to their salinity. Their composition is remarkably constant, though the chalybeates do vary slightly.

They are distributed in five main groups, but of these, three have had little influence on the growth of the town. The sulphur springs at Starbeck and Bilton Park are mentioned in the early seventeenth century: they failed to achieve subsequent prominence though baths were available at the former from 1822. The sulphur and chalybeate springs at Harlow Car, though known in the eighteenth century, were not actively exploited until the middle of the nineteenth, and this new spa was too remote from the town to be of much importance.

The remaining two groups have been the foci of development. The two chalybeate springs of High Harrogate, Tewit Well and St. John's Well, were the first to gain a reputation, and the early growth of the spa centred here. In the eighteenth century, however, Harrogate became increasingly noted for the efficacy of its sulphur water in the treatment of skin diseases. The Old Sulphur Well, in Low Harrogate, was used in this way at least as early as the beginning of the seventeenth century, and this area became the focus of later development. Its importance was enhanced when the variety of waters available here was realized. Both sulphur and chalybeate waters occur in close proximity in a rich profusion of springs: in Bogs Field alone, within an area of one acre, thirty-five distinct springs are found.

The distribution of the differing types of springs is not fortuitous, as they bear a close relation to the geological structure. The majority issue from, or near to, those outcrops of the Harrogate Roadstone series close to the axis of the Harrogate Anticline, especially where the fault to the north-west approaches the axis. Individual springs have locally independent sources: the water is at different levels in closely adjacent wells and pumping in one does not affect the height in the others. The springs nearest the axis of the Anticline have the highest mineral content, and in particular, the highest percentage of saline constituents. In this group are the majority of the Low Harrogate springs. Away from the axis are found such alkaline sulphur springs as those of Harlow Car, whilst on the margins of the area are pure chalybeates, best exemplified by the High Harrogate wells. There are some exceptions to this general grouping, in particular the occurrence of the chalybeate springs of Low Harrogate near the axis of the anticline. It has been suggested by R. G. S. Hudson that the water in these may have travelled in or under superficial deposits for some distance, and thus they have a surface outlet which is not coincident with their exit from the solid rocks.

The source and origin of these springs has occasioned much controversy, particularly during the nineteenth century, which it would be inappropriate to follow in detail. Certain significant facts emerge, however. The pure chalybeates show wide seasonal variations of temperature suggesting that they are simply percolating ground waters of meteoric origin. Such springs are common in other areas of the Millstone Grit, and their salts are derived from the leaching of the various beds of that formation. Their course is mainly in the joints and fault planes of the sandstones, and is not confined to areas of particular geological structures.

The temperature range of the saline sulphurs, on the other hand, is extremely small, suggesting that they have risen from considerable depths. These deep-seated springs reach the surface along the near-vertically disposed beds of the Anticline, and are separated from each other by the impervious beds of shale. Their detailed composition may well be a function of their depth of origin, though the source of their constituents is a matter for speculation. The most satisfactory explanation, advanced by R. G. S. Hudson in 1938, associated them with the existence of a minor oil pool within the structure of the Harrogate Anticline. In such a pool, the edge waters below the pool are of a saline nature. It is further suggested that sulphates in water in contact with oil are reduced to sulphides and sulphur, such a reaction being responsible for the sulphur and saline sulphur springs of the spa. The Bowland Shales, to which geological series the Harrogate Roadstones belong, are known to be rich in organic materials, and to contain traces of oil. An additional source of sulphides may be the various sulphur compounds within the shales. Confirmation of Hudson's hypothesis is partly provided by the existence of similar springs in the Carboniferous series of the eastern Pennines. A typical example is that at Aldfield, in the valley of the Skell 5 miles above Ripon.

One other facet of Harrogate's site remains for notice, its climate. Climate had virtually no part to play in the establishment of the spa, but its characteristics are not without interest. In general terms, Harrogate is typical of much of the western margins of the Vale of York. The rainfall is moderate, the area being within the rain shadow of the Pennines, and averages 30.51 in. per year. There is relatively little seasonal variation in rainfall, though there are pronounced peaks in July and August, and in October, with lower falls in the early spring and in September. The average temperatures are somewhat low, with an annual average of 47.1° F., a July average of 58.7° F. and a January average of 37.5° F. but this is due in part to the siting of the former recording station on Harlow Moor, 480 ft. above sea level. In terms of sunshine, Harrogate, with an annual average of 1342 hours, has one of the best records for the West Riding, but cannot compare in this respect with the majority of coastal resorts.

The general features of climate, however, are of little significance to the average visitor. Far more important is the bracing atmosphere associated with an exposed position on the flanks of the Pennines. In Professor Gordon Manley's words, 'Harrogate has an almost universal appeal as one of the most bracing inland resorts to be found'. This quality of the air cannot yet be measured, but it is universally experienced. George Eliot found the air 'delicious', whilst Southey wrote enthusiastically of 'a fine dry elastic air, so different from that of Keswick, that the difference is perceptible in breathing it ... the air would, I verily believe, give you new life'. Earlier reactions were not always so favourable. In the seventeenth century, Michael Stanhope complained that of patients to the spa, 'those that are weake ... receive more prejudice by the piercing bleake aire, than benefit by the water'.

In so far as this bracing atmosphere is associated with exposure, there are wide variations within the town. The bleakest areas are those around the Stray, whose open nature affords no effective wind-break. The trees planted along the roads at various times in the late eighteenth, and the nineteenth centuries, have changed to some extent the 'wild common, bare and bleak', of Smollett's time, but much of that quality remains. In contrast, the valley of Low Harrogate is far more sheltered, and the Valley Gardens distinctly relaxing in atmosphere.

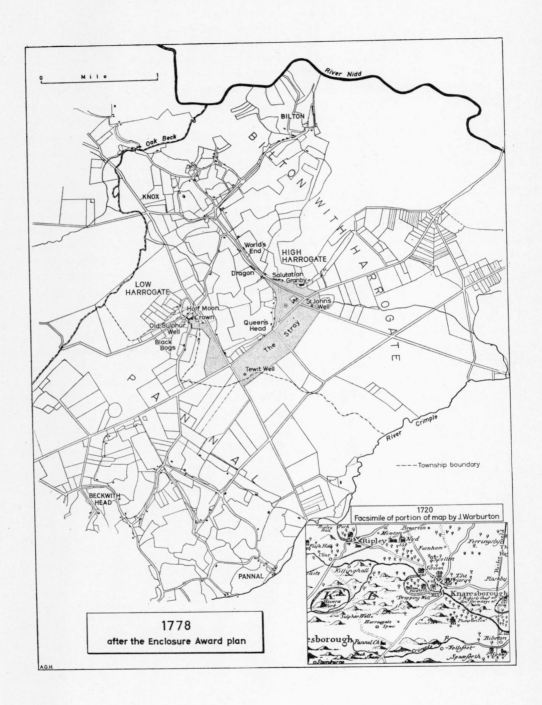

0 Mile 1

River Nidd

BILTON

BILTON WITH HARROGATE

Oak Beck

KNOX

World's End

HIGH HARROGATE

Dragon

Salutation
Granby

LOW HARROGATE

Half Moon
Crown

St Johns Well

Old Sulphur Well

Queen's Head

The Stray

Black Bogs

Tewit Well

PANNAL

River Crimple

------Township boundary

BECKWITH HEAD

1720
Facsimile of portion of map by J.Warburton

Ripley Hall Park
Flask Hall
Clint
Killinghall
Menton Brearton
Ripley Nyd
Farnham
Scotton Screven
Ferringsby Ha

Suite
Havera Park
K
B
The Priory
Knaresborough

Dropping Well

Sulphur Well
Harrogate Spaw

...esborough   Pannal Ch.
Crimple
Follyfoot
Spanforth
Stamburns

Plumpton Park
Report's Gaol and the wizards of
Leonard...
Ribston
B

1778
after the Enclosure Award plan

A.G.H.

12

4 Origins

THE oldest detailed map of Harrogate which has survived is this plan, which accompanied the Enclosure Award of 1778. Although its prime purpose was to show the allocation of land, it is a useful record of the extent of Georgian Harrogate. The settlement was still small and scattered at this date, but it had already been a spa for more than two centuries and something of its origins must now be traced.

Of Harrogate prior to the seventeenth century, very little is known. The earliest documentary evidence of the existence of a settlement distinct from the older villages of Bilton and Pannal is found in the Knaresborough Court Rolls of 1332. It was then, as it was to remain for more than three hundred years, a hamlet within the Forest of Knaresborough of no more than local importance. Almost certainly such settlement as existed was confined to the area later known as High Harrogate, and most likely consisted of scattered intakes from the Forest.

Harrogate's emergence as a spa can be dated from 1626, with the publication by Edmund Deane, a York doctor, of an account of its waters in his *Spadacrene Anglica, or the English Spaw Fountaine*, and by Michael Stanhope of a more popular description in his *Newes out of York-shire*. Deane also told of the first discovery of the waters 'about 55 yeares ago', in 1571, when William Slingsby, then living at 'a grange house very neare to this fountaine' and 'who drinking of this water found it in all things to agree with those at the Spaw' (i.e. the Belgian Spa) which he had visited in his youth. Slingsby's 'fountaine' was the chalybeate Tewit Well on the common land of High Harrogate, whose waters 'did excell the tart fountaines beyond the seas, as being more quick and lively, and fuller of minerall spirits'.

Deane devoted eleven of his sixteen chapters to the Tewit Well, but he also mentioned the sulphur springs in Bilton Park, at Starbeck and 'beyond a place called Haregate head, in a bottome on the right hand of it, as you goe, and almost in the side of a little brooke'. This last was the Old Sulphur Well; its offensive waters were used only by 'the vulgar sort', though it would appear that they had long been resorted to by the local people, and Deane commended their external use in the treatment of skin diseases.

Prior to the Restoration, the spa remained primitive. To the Tewit Well there was added the similar waters of St. John's Well, discovered in 1631, and sited on drier ground nearer to the existing settlement. The wells, however, were little more than unenclosed springs and the Forest itself was scarcely an attractive place. Stanhope wrote of 'a rude barren moore', and on his journey there in 1626 needed the services of a guide from Knaresborough. In 1697 Celia Fiennes could still complain that the whole of the area of the spa was 'all marshy and wette'. Like most visitors earlier in the century, she stayed in Knaresborough where, as Deane had been careful to note, 'there is nothing wanting, that may fitly serve for a good and commodious habitation, and the content and entertainment of strangers'.

Harrogate, indeed, was known as Knaresborough Spa throughout the seventeenth century, and its relatively undeveloped nature is still evident on Warburton's map of 1720. Stanhope wrote in 1632 that 'those who neighbour nearest to these waters are an indigenous poore people ... being plaine husbandmen and cottagers, and therefore it cannot be expected that they should accommodate them [i.e. the visitors]'. Improvement in this aspect came after the Restoration. The first inn, the Queen's Head, was opened in 1687, and it had been joined by the Dragon and the Granby before 1700, all significantly in High Harrogate.

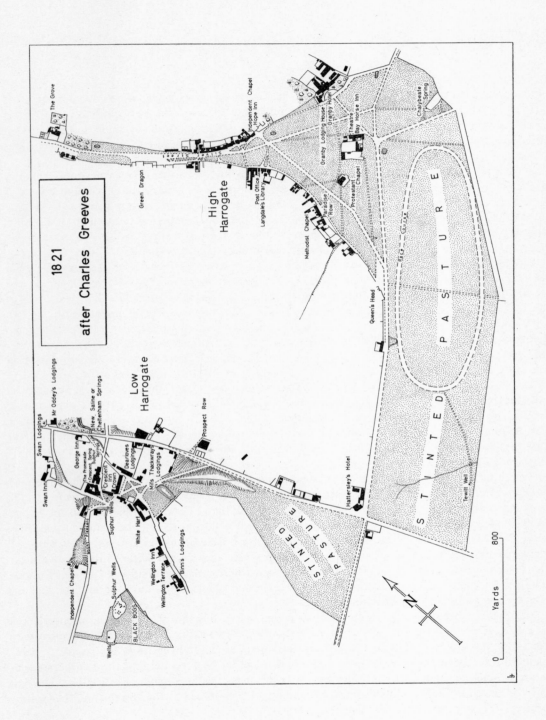

1821

after Charles Greeves

The Grove

Green Dragon

High Harrogate

Independent Chapel
Hope Inn

Post Office
Langdale's Library

Methodist Chapel

Paradise Row

Granby Lodging House
Granby Hotel

Theatre

Bay Horse Inn

Protestant Chapel

Chalybeate Spring

Swan Lodgings

Mr Oddey's Lodgings

New Saline or
Cheltenham Springs

Swan Inn

George Inn

The Promenade
Crescent Spring
Sulphur Springs

Crescent Inn
Crown

Dearloves
Lodgings

Mrs Thackwray's
Lodgings

Low Harrogate

Prospect Row

Sulphur Wells

White Hart

Wellington Inn

Wellington Terrace

Binn's Lodgings

Independent Chapel

Sulphur Wells

BLACK BOGS

Wells

Queen's Head

Hattersley's Hotel

Tewitt Well

S T I N T E D   P A S T U R E

S T I N T E D   P A S T U R E

N

Yards

0   800

14

5 Georgian and Regency villages

IN the early nineteenth century, a local surveyor, Charles Greeves, drew several plans of Harrogate of which the lithograph on which the accompanying map is based is perhaps the best known. It appears to have been drawn primarily to depict the Stray, or Stinted Pasture. Some of the fringing settlement is only shown schematically, but the map is nevertheless a most valuable record of the Regency spa.

Harrogate was still small, and rural in character. In 1801, the population of the township of Bilton-with-Harrogate (which included the village of Bilton but excluded that part of Low Harrogate lying within the parish of Pannal) was only 1195. Even in 1841, with a June census and the total swollen by early visitors, there were only 3372 persons. Nevertheless, the spa was markedly different from the primitive health resort of the pre-Restoration period. In medical terms, the prescribed regime was far less rigorous. The standard guide was T. Garnett's *Treatise on the Mineral Waters of Harrogate* (1792). The copious draughts advocated by Deane were replaced by recommended doses of three or four pints of chalybeate or up to two pints of sulphur water with, in both cases, a respite of 10 minutes or more between glasses. Patients were no longer peremptorily commanded to exercise, but were more gently urged that 'early rising being conducive to health in general, and to the successful use of this water in particular, I would advise invalids to repair to the wells early in the morning, and drink the water at the fountain head'.

Even more revealing were some of Garnett's general comments. 'Among the advantages [of Harrogate as a spa]', he wrote, 'we must not forget the sociability of the company.' Even dancing, 'a more laborious kind of exercise', could be recommended. When 'enjoyed with moderation ... it may in some diseases prove not only harmless, but beneficial'. One suspects more than a grain of truth in the plaint of the writer of 1812 who

> ... sat down
> With a number of invalid folks at the Crown,
> But what way invalid to unfold I'm not able,
> Unless 'tis with cramming at Thackwray's good table.

In these changes, Harrogate was no different from the other spas of the period. The wells still had a vital part to play in its life and their location greatly influenced the direction of growth of the settlement, and the changing fortunes of High and Low Harrogate. Early development had favoured High Harrogate, with its chalybeate springs, but these were increasingly neglected in favour of the sulphur waters of Low Harrogate. Deane had noted the Old Sulphur Well in 1626, and Celia Fiennes visited it in 1697, but the use of its waters had been hindered by the lack of accommodation, and of suitable baths for their external application. The change in fortune came in 1740, when Joseph Thackrey established the Crown Hotel immediately adjacent to the well: by the end of the century, Harrogate water and the Old Sulphur Well were synonymous.

Nor was this the only well in use: the real advantage of Low Harrogate lay in its profusion of springs of varying character. The potentialities of Black Bogs, or Bogs Field, had been recognized in the seventeenth century. Even more important was the discovery of two additional springs in immediate proximity to the Old Well itself, which were used to provide supplies of water for

15

bathing. From the end of the eighteenth century, three new areas were developed. One was in the north-west of the present Crescent Gardens. In 1783, the landlord of the Half Moon Inn (subsequently the Crescent, and now demolished), in digging for water behind the house, encountered by chance a new sulphur spring, and, in 1790, discovered a chalybeate spring, the Crescent Saline, in the cellar of his house. A second area was in the Montpellier Gardens, immediately east of the Crown Hotel and purchased by Thackrey in 1765. From 1810 several springs were discovered here, three in particular being used for drinking and treatment, the Strong and Mild Montpellier Sulphurs and the Kissingen Saline Chalybeate. A third area lay to the east of the Ripon road near the site of the present Royal Hall where the Chloride of Iron and Pure Chalybeates were found in 1818.

Facilities for using these waters did not proliferate with their discovery. Throughout the eighteenth century, bathing was confined entirely to the hotels and lodging houses, and the wells themselves were the only facilities possessed by the spa. Nevertheless, the worst features were gradually removed, and Garnett could not 'forbear congratulating the company at Harrogate, on the abolition of the absurd and indelicate customs formerly in use'.

The rise in the importance of the Low Harrogate springs was not immediately matched by a corresponding rise in the importance of that part of the settlement in other directions. High Harrogate remained the commercial and social centre long after its wells had ceased to be of prime significance. Its impetus came from its initial possession of the major hotels of the spa: surprisingly enough, the three in existence by 1700 remained almost unique, the only addition of any importance being the Salutation, or the Hope Inn and Gascoigne's Hotel as it successively became. Additional accommodation was provided in many of the dwellings lining the Stray, which became lodging houses during the season.

The social prestige of High Harrogate was reinforced by its commercial supremacy. *Baines's Directory* of 1822 lists 35 shopkeepers in Harrogate: of these only 3 were in Low Harrogate. The principal shops lined Regent Parade and Park Parade. Several only opened for the season, and contemporary advertisements stressed their intimate connections with London firms. They became almost as much social as commercial rendezvous, a role which they shared with the two libraries. Another place of assembly was the theatre. This was opened in 1788 on a site in Church Square, but Harrogate was not really large enough to give it adequate support: it eventually closed in the 1830s, being converted into two dwellings which still remain as Mansfield House. In High Harrogate, too, was the spa's first church. The chapel of St. John was built by public subscription, and was opened in 1749. It rapidly became inadequate for the growing number of visitors, and was replaced on the same site in 1831 by the present Christ Church.

Harrogate lacked completely the formal promenades of more developed spas. In their place, however, was the open common called the Stray, which still gives the town so much of its character. Initially a portion of the Forest of Knaresborough over which common grazing rights were enjoyed, it was a distinctive feature mentioned in many early accounts and permitting free access to the first wells. Its contribution to the life of the spa was recognized in the Act of Enclosure of 1770, when it was preserved as an unenclosed stinted pasture in order that 'all persons whomsoever shall and may have access at all times to the said springs, and be at liberty to use and drink the waters there arising, and take the benefit thereof, and shall and may have use, and enjoy full and free ingress, egress, and regress in, upon, and over the said two hundred acres of land'. Although the Stray extended as far as Low Harrogate, it was of benefit primarily to High Harrogate. In 1793, a racecourse was laid out here to add to existing amenities.

Plate V. The Regency Spa

(*a*) The Montpellier Baths, erected in 1835 and demolished about 1890. Chromolithograph by W. Monkhouse, York.

(*b*) The Spa Rooms, formerly the Cheltenham Pump Room, erected in 1835 and demolished in 1939. Chromolithograph by W. Monkhouse, York.

Plate VI. The Advent of the Railway

(a) The Crimple viaduct of the York and North Midland Railway's branch to Harrogate. An 1847 lithograph by Gibson & Co., York, of 'this stupendous work now erecting'.

(b) A photograph taken shortly after the opening in 1862 of the linking line through Central Harrogate. The then completely open nature of the area is striking. The overbridge crosses Bower Road, and is still extant, whilst Oxford Street is in the foreground.

Plate VII. Life in Victorian Harrogate

(*a*) Prospect Hill about 1890. The bath chair rank is prominent.

(*b*) The Valley Gardens about 1900.

Plate VIII. Victorian Street Scenes

(*a*) Parliament Street about 1890, before the Royal Hall was built in the valley beyond.

(*b*) James Street, about 1900.

The Stray gave form to High Harrogate: the houses lined it on two sides, jostling for a frontage as on a seaside promenade. In the eighteenth century, the houses were thinly scattered, but in the early nineteenth century most of the intervening spaces were filled. Leading off from the Stray frontage were several small courts, but these were nowhere on an extensive scale.

Low Harrogate was far more amorphous in layout. Until the mid-nineteenth century virtually the only buildings, apart from a few cottages, were the hotels. Of these, the doyen was the Crown, the only one also of a social status to compare with the High Harrogate trio. Close to it, in the floor of the valley, were the White Hart, the Crescent, the Promenade and the Swan, and to the south-west up Cold Bath Road were the Wellington and Binns'. The social distinctions long persisted. As late as 1839, when Dr. Granville visited the spa, they were still sufficiently evident to arouse his attention. The increasing numbers of 'opulent Leeds, Sheffield and Manchester factors' patronized the Low Harrogate hotels — the Swan, the White Hart, the Wellington or 'summum bonum, the Crown'. The last was also the choice of the aristocratic invalid who wished to be close to the waters. In contrast, 'the Dragon and the Granby were sacred places. The Lords only graced the latter, while the wealthy commoner pleased himself in the former'.

The pattern of life in the spa at this period lacked the precise formality of the larger spas of the south, and in the absence of formal assembly rooms, centred on the inns. To some extent, this led to the lack of a close-knit community such as was the essential feature of the Bath of Beau Nash, but it was partly mitigated by the holding of communal evening balls at the principal hotels. In 1816, there were weekly balls at the Dragon, the Crown, the Queen's Head and the Granby, with private dances on the remaining evenings. Invitations were sent from each hotel to the other, so that all guests might meet on these occasions.

The daily routine followed an ordered pattern. The day began early with a visit to the wells. For those resident in High Harrogate, quite a journey was necessary. The majority went by carriage, an indulgence that would have grieved Deane deeply. The procedure of drinking occupied an hour or more — the usual draught was three pints with an interval of walking between each glass — and the company then returned to their respective hotels for breakfast. The rest of the day was spent in varied pursuits. True invalids would use the water for bathing two or three times a week. The spa itself afforded varied diversions. The Stray, with its fringing shops and libraries, was the principal promenade, whilst many of the company preferred to leave Harrogate for excursions to neighbouring beauty spots and places of interest. The unsophisticated atmosphere of the spa was everywhere evident: its spirit was aptly caught by the author of *John Buncle* when he declared in 1756 that 'with the greatest civility, cheerfulness and good humour, there is a certain rural plainness and freedom mixed, which are vastly pleasing'.

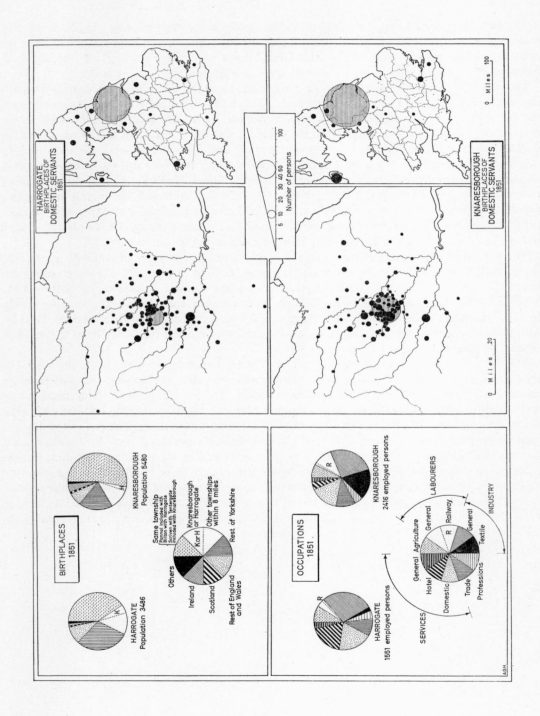

HARROGATE
BIRTHPLACES OF
DOMESTIC SERVANTS
1851

KNARESBOROUGH
BIRTHPLACES OF
DOMESTIC SERVANTS
1851

Number of persons

100 40 50 30 20 10 5 1

0 Miles 100

0 Miles 20

BIRTHPLACES
1851

KNARESBOROUGH
Population 5480

HARROGATE
Population 3486

Some township
(Fennel included with
Bilton with Harrogate
Scriven with Tentergate
included with Knaresborough)

Knaresborough
K or H Harrogate

Others

Other townships
within 8 miles

Ireland

Scotland

Rest of Yorkshire

Rest of England
and Wales

OCCUPATIONS
1851

KNARESBOROUGH
2416 employed persons

HARROGATE
1551 employed persons

SERVICES

General Agriculture

Hotel

General R Railway

Domestic

R

LABOURERS

General

Trade

Professions

Textile

General

INDUSTRY

A.G.H.

18

6 The mid-nineteenth Century

AT the beginning of the Victorian era, Harrogate was on the threshold of dramatic changes. After 1851, its rate of growth quickened markedly: in the ensuing 60 years its population increased by 916 per cent. The magnitude of these changes is seen more clearly when Harrogate is compared with its neighbouring market town, Knaresborough. The latter, like many long-established small towns at this period, remained virtually stagnant. Between 1851 and 1911, in fact, its population actually decreased by 4 per cent. It had made a bid for industrial prosperity in the eighteenth century, with the development of a linen industry, but it was too far to the north of the West Riding coalfield to maintain that prosperity with the advent of mechanization and of steam power. It was not surpassed in size by Harrogate until the 1860s, but could not subsequently compare with its vigorous neighbour.

Some of the contrasts between the towns are illustrated on these maps, compiled from the enumerators' books of the 1851 Census. The books enable far more detail to be obtained than is possible from the published census returns alone.

With the fundamentally different functions of the towns in 1851, contrasts in occupations are naturally striking. The railway labourers at Knaresborough represent an ephemeral element in the occupational structure. There were 245 in the town, more than 10 per cent of the total occupied persons, and they were engaged in the completion of the railway viaduct. More important was the large proportion still engaged in textile manufacture. Despite the decline of the linen industry, it still provided 18 per cent of the employment in the town. In Harrogate, hotel staffs formed 19 per cent of the total employed. The significance of this figure is increased when it is remembered that those so employed were not always specifically distinguished by the enumerators.

In other occupations the towns were more comparable. Harrogate had a greater number engaged in industry but the total was inflated by the large number of stone-masons in the rapidly growing town. Knaresborough had a greater proportion of craft industries. Knaresborough also had a slightly higher percentage engaged in trade, a reflection of a commercial supremacy which was not to persist for long.

The data on birthplaces gives some clues as to the origins of the population. The contrasts between the towns are not perhaps as marked as one might expect. Knaresborough had 53 per cent of its population born within the same township, and an additional 14 per cent within 8 miles. For Harrogate, the comparable figures were 41 per cent and 14 per cent, surprisingly high for a rapidly expanding settlement. The element of comparison is heightened when the figures for the percentages born in Yorkshire as a whole are considered: Knaresborough had 87 per cent and Harrogate 88 per cent. In neither town, therefore, was there much attraction to movement from beyond Yorkshire, though Harrogate naturally drew from a wider local field than its neighbour, a trend further illustrated by the maps of the birthplaces of the domestic servants working in each. These figures emphasize that Harrogate's importance was still relatively limited in extent. One important ephemeral element in the Knaresborough figures must be mentioned. The high proportion born in Ireland was due largely to the presence of the railway labourers.

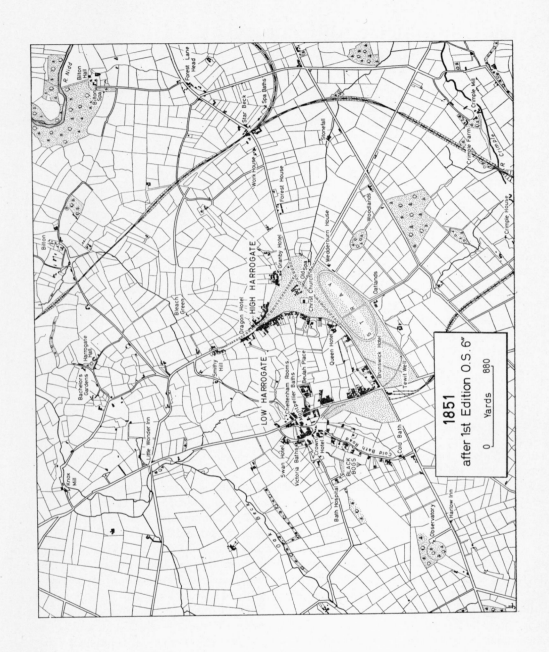

1851
after 1st Edition O.S. 6"

Yards
0   880

7 The Threshold of Change

THE rapid expansion of Harrogate in the Victorian era can be attributed to two particular causes. The importance of improved access will be discussed in the next section, but of equal significance were conscious endeavours to improve the facilities at the spa, enabling Harrogate to share to the full in the general revival of interest in spas in the latter half of the nineteenth century.

The Victorian spa depended on more than the favour of fashion and the availability of springs. The Cure became increasingly complex, and the physical treatments which became associated with it needed suites of baths and other facilities. Harrogate's early deficiencies in this respect have already been noted, but they were remedied to some extent by private enterprise in the 1830s. The earliest development was on land adjacent to the Crescent Hotel, where a promenade room was built in 1805. This was superseded in 1832 by the building of John Williams's baths, or the Victoria Baths as they subsequently became, a curious building with an Ionic front, and built into the ground as the tenant was precluded from raising a building on it. The rival establishment was the Montpellier Baths, built in 1835 on Thackwray's land. This was an elegant building, with twelve tile-lined baths, and a central hall where bathers were entertained by a band each morning. It was apparently better patronized than its slightly older rival. In 1839, Dr. Granville recorded that the Victoria Baths were giving 4000 baths each season, and the Montpellier 6000. Social amenities were enhanced by the opening in 1835 of the Royal Promenade and Cheltenham Pump Room. The largest public building in Harrogate, its elegant Doric portico made it one of the very few erections in the spa with any architectural distinction. It contained a large saloon, a pump room and a library, and subscribers had, in addition, access to 6 acres of gardens. It was demolished in 1939.

All these developments, significantly, took place in close proximity in Low Harrogate, the centre of the Victorian spa, and proved to be the impetus towards the municipal provision of facilities which was to be the keystone of Victorian prosperity. The hoteliers who had no share in these private spas were naturally anxious to preserve public access to the wells, and to develop public amenities for the benefit of their own visitors. Together with a group of other leading townspeople similarly interested in perpetuating the public ownership of the wells, they secured the passage of the Harrogate Improvement Act in 1841, and the creation of a body of Improvement Commissioners.

The Act laid the foundations of the municipal development of the spa, although the powers of the Commissioners were relatively limited. In their initial enthusiasm, they concentrated on improving the facilities at existing public wells. The Old Sulphur Well was the natural object of their attention, and in 1842 the present Royal Pump Room was completed at a cost of £3000. The pre-existing cover erected in 1804 was transferred to the Tewit Well, where it still remains. A new cover was also built over St. John's Well in 1842. After this initial activity, the Commissioners relapsed into matters of routine concern for a considerable period, but their very existence was the key to the later development of the spa. Harrogate now possessed not only the form of a town, but the rudiments of effective urban government.

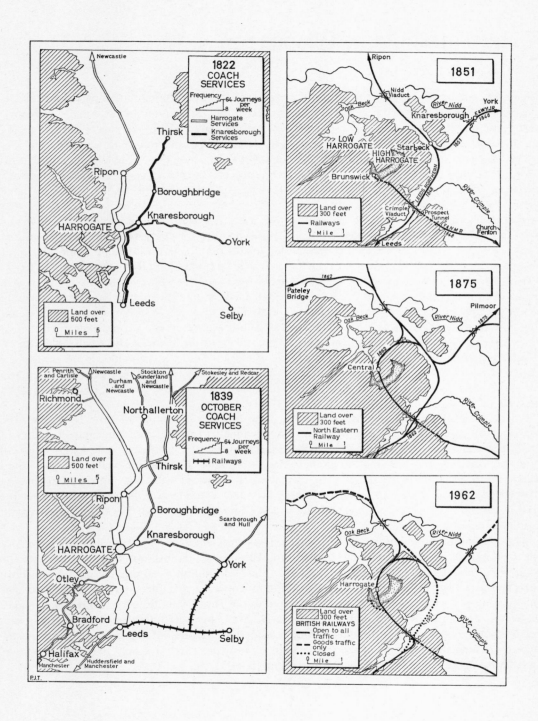

1822 COACH SERVICES

Frequency
64 Journeys per week
8

Harrogate Services
Knaresborough Services

Newcastle
Thirsk
Ripon
Boroughbridge
Knaresborough
HARROGATE
York
Leeds
Selby

Land over 500 feet

0 Miles 5

1851

Ripon
Nidd Viaduct
Oak Beck
River Nidd
York
Knaresborough
E&WYJR 1848
LOW HARROGATE
Starbeck
HIGH HARROGATE
LEEDS NORTHERN 1848
Brunswick
River Crimple
Crimple Viaduct
Prospect Tunnel
Y&NMR 1848
Church Fenton
Leeds

Land over 300 feet
Railways
0 Mile

1875

1862
Pateley Bridge
Oak Beck
River Nidd
1875
Pilmoor
1862
Central
River Crimple
1862

Land over 300 feet
North Eastern Railway
0 Mile

1839 OCTOBER COACH SERVICES

Frequency
64 Journeys per week
8
Railways

Penrith and Carlisle
Newcastle
Stockton Sunderland and Newcastle
Stokesley and Redcar
Durham and Newcastle
Richmond
Northallerton
Land over 500 feet
0 Miles 5
Thirsk
Ripon
Boroughbridge
Scarborough and Hull
Knaresborough
HARROGATE
York
Otley
Bradford
Leeds
Selby
Halifax
Manchester
Huddersfield and Manchester

1962

Oak Beck
River Nidd
1875
Harrogate
1851
River Crimple

Land over 300 feet
BRITISH RAILWAYS
Open to all traffic
Goods traffic only
Closed
0 Mile

P.J.T.

22

8 The Advent of the Railway

THE increased wealth brought by the Industrial Revolution gave rise to a new clientele for the spa in the *nouveaux riches* of the West Riding, but improvements in the means of access were necessary before they could come in large numbers.

Existing road transport was unsuitable in this respect. There was a coach from Leeds at least as early as 1743, and by the late 1830s there were ten running each day between Harrogate and Leeds, even out of season. Harrogate also benefited by its position on the main route from Leeds to Ripon and Newcastle.

The spa was not large enough to attract early railway promoters: the country was difficult for construction and seasonal passenger traffic alone would not justify the building of a line. In the speculative atmosphere of the Railway Mania of the 1840s, conditions were very different; between 1848 and 1851, three separate routes were completed to the infant spa. The branch of George Hudson's York and North Midland Railway, opened on 20 July 1848, followed a high-level approach from the east. It necessitated considerable engineering works, including the $\frac{3}{4}$-mile Prospect Tunnel, followed almost immediately by a 31-arch viaduct 110 ft. high over the Crimple valley. Further cuttings, and another short tunnel, brought the line to a terminus in West Park, opposite the Brunswick Hotel (later the Prince of Wales). At the same time, the Leeds and Thirsk Railway was promoted, passing through Harrogate, although its prime purpose was to challenge Hudson's monopoly north of York. Opened on 13 September 1848, it chose a low-level route, following the valley of the Crimple and skirting Harrogate on the north. Starbeck was chosen as one of the principal locomotive depots, a status it retained until 1959 when the locomotive sheds were closed. The third route was of lesser importance. The East and West Yorkshire Junction Railway was a locally promoted link between Starbeck and York, and after several vicissitudes, was opened throughout on 1 October 1851.

Although Harrogate now possessed railways in full measure, the benefits were far from complete. Brunswick station was reasonably convenient for both High and Low Harrogate, but it was the terminus of a branch which gave only indirect access to the industrial West Riding. The station at Starbeck, though served by direct routes to Leeds, York and north-east England, was inconveniently sited for the spa. Omnibuses meeting every train could not completely compensate for its isolation, and road coaches were still running between Harrogate and Leeds in 1851.

In 1854, all the railways in the area came under the control of the North Eastern Railway. The new company soon sought to remove anomalies by connecting the existing lines and providing a new central station. Despite much local opposition to 'thundering trains rushing across our quiet fields and pleasant footpaths', as the *Harrogate Advertiser* phrased it, the new line was opened on 1 August 1862, running through the still open ground between High and Low Harrogate. Henceforth all passenger trains used this route. The site of Brunswick station, which had been closed almost immediately, was given to the town for incorporation in the Stray, as compensation for the land taken from it in constructing the new route. The effect of these changes was immediate: it could certainly be claimed, in the words of an observer of 1899, that 'it was the railway coming to Harrogate that made Harrogate, not Harrogate coming to the railway'.

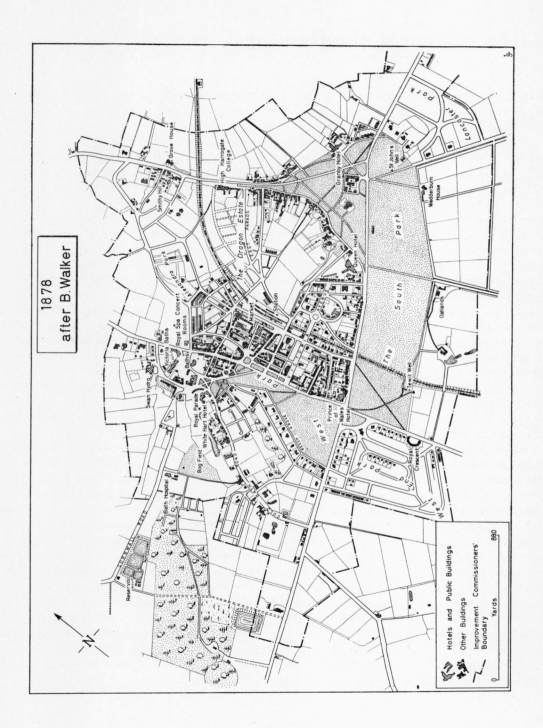

1878
after B.Walker

Hotels and Public Buildings
Other Buildings
Improvement Commissioners'
Boundary

0   880
Yards

9 Victorian Spa

HARROGATE'S status as a town was formally recognized by its incorporation as a Borough in 1884. As a spa it not only survived but prospered. The treatment centre of the Victorian spa was a far cry from the pump room of the eighteenth century. Capital for the development of facilities was not easy to acquire, but in Harrogate it was forthcoming as the conscious result of municipal policy.

The foundations of this policy were laid by the Improvement Commissioners. In 1868, they began a programme of expansion which by the end of the century brought the whole of the spa area of Low Harrogate under municipal ownership, and furnished it with unequalled facilities amongst British spas. Their first acquisition was the Crescent Hotel, and the adjacent Victoria Baths: these were replaced in 1871 by the building of the new Victoria Baths, on the site of the present Municipal Offices.

The work was continued by the newly created Borough Council. In 1888, they bought the Montpellier estate, and they began construction on this site of the extensive Royal Baths, completed in 1897 at a cost of £118,000. The new building, though undistinguished architecturally, was lavishly equipped. Other amenities were not neglected. In 1896, the remaining private spa, the Cheltenham Spa Rooms, was acquired, and in 1903 the new Kursaal was opened on an adjacent site. The latter was renamed the Royal Hall in 1914, when emulation of the German spas was no longer popular. In the valley above the Old Sulphur Well, the extensive informal parade of the Valley Gardens was laid out. The area had apparently been used as a public open space for many years prior to the creation of the Borough, but the land was purchased by the Corporation in 1886, and opened as the Valley Gardens in 1887. In 1898, part of Harlow Moor to the west was purchased, and in 1901 Collins's Field, lying between the Valley Gardens and Cornwall Road to the north. The other great amenity, the Stray, was also brought under Municipal ownership. The grazing rights of the 'proprietors' were bought by the Corporation in 1893, and a programme of tree-planting and other improvements begun.

Visitors came in increasing numbers. The now largely middle-aged and elderly clientele of the spa was still socially distinct, if no longer so virile as in earlier years. In August 1898, 52,851 glasses of spa water were served, 31,546 at the Royal Pump Room, 12,757 within the Royal Bath, and 8448 at the Magnesia Well in the Valley Gardens. In the same month, 18,723 baths were given, 11,984 at the Royal Baths. Inevitably, with such numbers, the intimate atmosphere of earlier years almost completely disappeared. Some former customs were retained, however, such as the early morning drinking of the waters. On a single morning in August 1901, 1800 visitors were served with water at the Royal Pump Room between 7 and 9 a.m. Congestion here was such that an annexe was added to the Pump Room in 1913.

But Harrogate was not solely a spa. Its commercial importance was growing and, like Cheltenham, it attracted several private schools. Increasingly, it became a dormitory town for Leeds and the West Riding. Such changes were not always welcome. A witness at the Borough Extension Inquiry in 1899 said of new houses on the Duchy Estate that they were occupied primarily by Leeds and Bradford business men, 'a good class of house ... and a poor class of people live in them'.

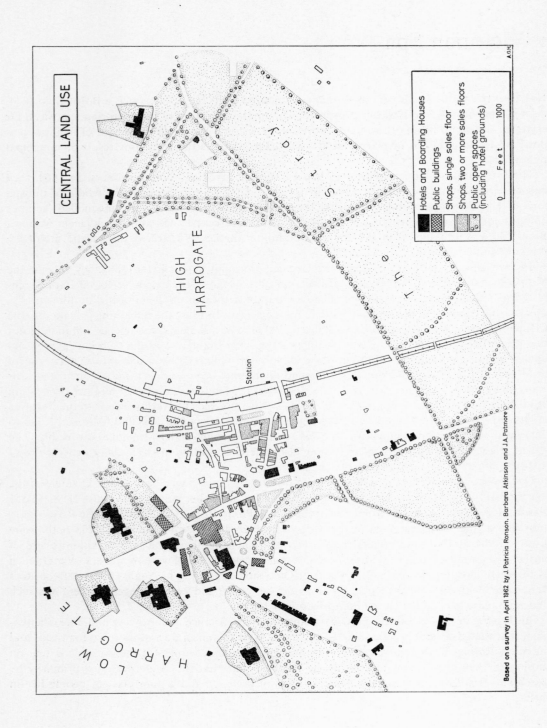

CENTRAL LAND USE

HIGH HARROGATE

LOW HARROGATE

The Stray

Station

Hotels and Boarding Houses
Public buildings
Shops, single sales floor
Shops, two or more sales floors
Public open spaces (including hotel grounds)

0   Feet   1000

Based on a survey in April 1962 by J. Patricia Ronson, Barbara Atkinson and J.A. Patmore

26

10 The changing Town Centre

THE twin villages of Regency Harrogate were transformed in more ways than one by the advent of the railway. The linking line of 1862 had passed through what was still open ground between the villages, but the new station provided a new focus for development. As by now the spa facilities were concentrated in Low Harrogate, the streets leading to it from the station acquired a new importance, and rapidly developed as the commercial centre of the town. This rise of central Harrogate was matched by the decline of the former commercial supremacy of High Harrogate.

Today, the commercial area is still distinct, sandwiched between the railway and the spa area as such. The earliest shops were opened along Parliament Street, leading down the side of the valley to the spa. It was soon joined by James Street, which completed the route to the station. These two streets, and James Street in particular, still contain the most exclusive shops in the town, notably those for jewellery and clothing. The main banks also cluster in James Street and around Prospect Square. North of James Street, and parallel to it, Cambridge Street and Chapel Street developed later, and were by no means exclusive. The Improvement Commissioners established their market on a site in Cambridge Street in 1874, where its successor still stands. This street is also notable for branches of several multiple retail firms.

The evolution of the spa area as such has already been considered: closely associated with it in location and function were the hotels. In the period of railway construction, many existing hotels were enlarged and rebuilt. The White Hart, for example, was rebuilt in 1846, the Crown in 1847 and 1870, the George in 1850, Prospect House in 1859 and 1870 and the Brunswick in 1860. There was no major change in location, although the tendency for the hotels to congregate either in Low Harrogate, or along the fringes of the Stray in Central Harrogate, was increased. In High Harrogate, not only were there no new hotels, but the one furthest from the Stray, the Dragon, became a school in this period and was subsequently demolished.

There was renewed activity after the creation of the Borough. In part, this was a continuation of earlier trends, with the rebuilding of existing properties. In November 1898, for example, plans were handed in for extensions to the following hotels, the Queen and the Granby in High Harrogate, the Alexandra in Central Harrogate, and the Crown and the Adelphi in Low Harrogate. Even more important was the great increase in new construction in Low Harrogate. Rows of terrace boarding houses were built, particularly along Valley Drive, where many still form hotels, Cheltenham Parade and Cheltenham Crescent. On the north side of the Low Harrogate valley, in an area where previously the Swan had been almost the only building, three vast new hotels arose, the Majestic, the Cairn Hydro and the Grand, each set in extensive grounds. Thus Low Harrogate developed almost exclusively as a resort area, with the municipal spa at its core, and surrounded on almost every side by different types of accommodation. Few shops exist here, and many of these are closely associated with the resort function. It is not coincidence that the majority of the numerous antique shops for which Harrogate is famous are found in Low or High Harrogate, and not in the later commercial centre of the town.

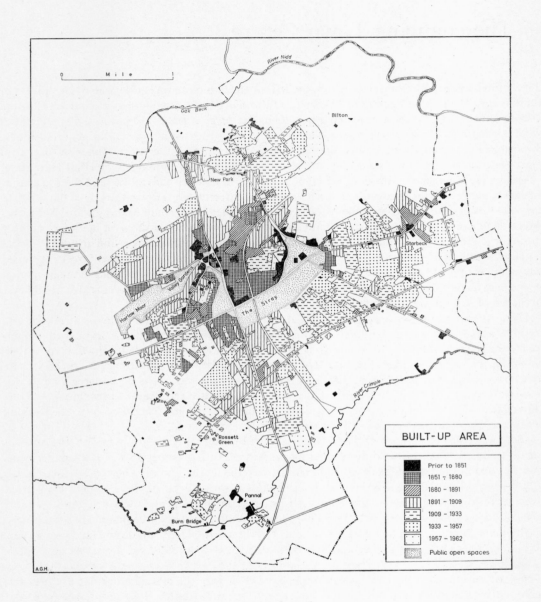

BUILT-UP AREA

Prior to 1851
1851 - 1880
1880 - 1891
1891 - 1909
1909 - 1933
1933 - 1957
1957 - 1962
Public open spaces

River Nidd

Bilton

Oak Beck

New Park

Starbeck

Valley Gardens

Harlow Moor

The Stray

River Crimple

Rossett Green

Pannal

Burn Bridge

0   Mile   1

A.G.H.

28

11 Residential Expansion

THE centre of Harrogate is still stolidly Victorian in aspect, a trait which belongs as much to its houses as to the shops and hotels. Between 1851 and 1880, development was in three main areas, between High Harrogate and Central Harrogate, in West End Park, and to the west of the Stray. Development in the first of these areas was largely by a single company, the Victoria Park Company. With a capital of £28,000, a large plot of land was bought in 1860, and laid out with broad roads, and building lots offered for sale. Victoria Avenue in particular remains as a witness to the effectiveness of the scheme, although many of the residential properties to the west of the railway have now been converted to other uses. West End Park was a similar company development dating from 1867. Seventy acres south of the Stray were purchased from the North Eastern Railway, and laid out in a formal oval. Miniature mansions exhibiting to the full the vagaries of Victorian style began to be built on the various lots. The initial advertisement of the sites took care to stress that the estate was 'free from SMOKE, DUST and NOISE of Railway Traffic, narrow streets and back lanes, and houses of the Cottage Class, which have been studiously avoided'. Houses of similar scale and magnificence were built along Beech Grove, fronting West Park Stray.

The social contrasts of residential development were accentuated after 1880. To the north, on both sides of the railway, the Alexandra Park and Dragon Estates were rapidly built over. The great majority of houses were of a terrace type, many quite substantial in design but others showing the poorer features of Victorian 'byelaw' housing. After 1900, this type of development spread beyond Skipton Road, in New Park and towards Bilton. West of Ripon Road, and south of the Stray along Leeds Road, housing was of a far more substantial nature. This was particularly true of the area between the Valley Gardens and Oak Beck, which between 1891 and 1909 was quickly covered with detached residences of considerable size.

The Victorian period in Harrogate left a legacy of layout and style which was admirable in many features, the broad, tree-lined roads in particular. Post-1918 Harrogate, on the other hand, has less to distinguish it from the suburbs of many other English towns. The rapid expansion in area has been greatest on the eastern side, east of Leeds Road and Ripon Road. Corporation development has been largely in the north and east of the semi-circle. New Park has become a major suburb, and council estates stretch almost to the railway at Bilton. Bilton village, however, the original parent settlement, is still a small rural community with virtually no modern buildings. Between Bilton and Starbeck, a wedge of open land still reaches almost to the Granby in High Harrogate, but it is succeeded by a rapidly expanding area of housing development on both sides of Knaresborough Road. Estates are now being built to the east of the railway at Starbeck.

West of Wetherby Road, and along both sides of Leeds Road, development has been mainly in private hands, with much interdigitation of pre- and post-war building. The area south of the Stray was first used for development between the wars: Wedderburn House, isolated since its construction by Lord Loughborough in 1786, is now almost swamped by new construction, its former extensive grounds curtailed to a small garden. Along the northern crest of the Crimple valley, and extending through Rossett Green to Pannal and Burn Bridge, are the largest modern houses, though few compare in size with their Victorian predecessors.

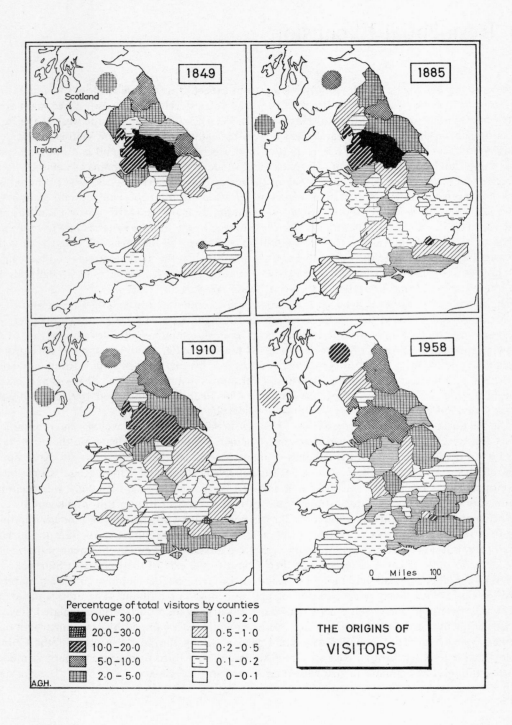

Percentage of total visitors by counties

- Over 30·0
- 20·0 – 30·0
- 10·0 – 20·0
- 5·0 – 10·0
- 2·0 – 5·0
- 1·0 – 2·0
- 0·5 – 1·0
- 0·2 – 0·5
- 0·1 – 0·2
- 0 – 0·1

THE ORIGINS OF
VISITORS

AGH.

30

12 Visitors

HARROGATE without its visitors is indeed Hamlet without the Prince. It is fortunate that sufficient evidence has survived to enable both their actual numbers and their places of origin to be traced back to the eighteenth century.

The earliest record comes from Hargrove, the Knaresborough historian, writing in 1798. He noted 1556 visitors during the 1781 season, and 2458 'exclusive of servants' in 1795. It is difficult to estimate what these figures mean in terms of numbers actually visiting the spa at any one time, but it seems reasonable to assume weekly totals of perhaps 200 and 350 respectively at the height of the season in these years. By 1810, numbers had more than doubled, for in that year the Rev. Robert Mitton, the curate of Harrogate, recorded 5858 arrivals in the season. From 1828, the more precise evidence of the weekly visitors' lists is available. For a week in September 1828, 713 visitors were in the town, 430 in hotels and 283 in private lodgings. High Harrogate's share of the total was 280, 192 being in hotels.

Prior to Victorian times, there is no precise evidence as to the places from which the visitors came, and contemporary accounts are too vague for any accurate impression to be obtained. Such fragments as do exist support Smollett's impression in 1785 that 'the majority are of the northern counties, and many come from Scotland for the benefit of these waters'. They belonged essentially to the rural areas, and to the older northern towns. The unsophisticated spa had little appeal to metropolitan society, but as the nineteenth century advanced it attracted increasing numbers of those who owed their wealth to the Industrial Revolution. A correspondent of Dr. Granville's, writing in July 1839, disparagingly remarked that Harrogate was 'as yet, full of clothiers from Leeds, and cutlers from Sheffield'. For August the prospects were brighter, 'Sheffield and Leeds will soon loom homewards, and then, they say, better company will come'.

From 1849, the visitors' lists contain not only the names but also the normal residences of visitors, and it is from this data that the first three of the accompanying maps have been compiled., Numbers rapidly increased as the spa expanded. For a September week in 1849, 1911 are recorded with 1033 of these in lodgings — virtually 2000 visitors weekly in a town with a resident population of less than 3500. High Harrogate's share of the total had declined to a quarter. By 1863, 62,212 visitors were listed in the course of the year, and, allowing for the fact that many stayed longer than a week, about 30,000 visitors were coming to Harrogate annually. More than 2500 were accommodated each week at the height of the season. In August Bank Holiday Week, 1885, 3638 visitors were entered in the lists, and for the same week in 1910 the total had risen to 6238. The latter figure suggests an annual total of at least 75,000 visitors.

In early Victorian times, Harrogate was still a north country spa. At the height of the 1849 season, for the week in September which the map represents, the majority of the visitors were from the industrial areas of the West Riding, Lancashire and the north-east. Access was still a problem, and very few visitors made a journey of more than 85 miles. By 1885, changes were becoming evident. The industrial north was still the most important contributor, but increasing numbers were coming from further afield. This trend had become even more marked by Edwardian times as is clearly shown on the map of the sample list of 1910. Particularly noticeable is the decreased share of the West Riding, and the increased numbers from south-east England. More than one in eight of all visitors were now coming from London itself. This is an indication of a most important change, of the northern spa accepted by metropolitan society. It was indeed a particularly useful place to stay between the end of the London season, and the beginning of grouse shooting from Scottish country seats. The change in social status was reflected in the titled visitors of Edwardian days. The town had hopefully erected a statue of Victoria in her golden jubilee year, but that Queen did not give Harrogate the stimulus of her physical presence. It was, in consequence, a real triumph when, on an August day in 1911, there were no less than three queens in the spa, Queen Alexandra, Empress Marie of Russia and Queen Amelie of Portugal. These were far from the only royal visitors in what was a vintage year in this respect!

The maps apply to resident visitors, but they were not the only category. Day trippers came in increasing numbers. 'A Leeds poet' of 1890 coined these lines of doggerel:

> The joyful Sabbath comes, that blessed day,
> When all seem happy, and where all seem gay,
> Then toil hath ceased, and then both rich and poor,
> Fly off to Harrogate or Woodhouse Moor.

Such an influx was not accepted happily by the Victorian spa. In 1867, the *Harrogate Herald* called attention to 'the nuisance created by persons who come to Harrogate in omnibuses and other vehicles on Sundays, and congregate in the neighbourhood of Tower Street and West Park, to the annoyance of respectable visitors and inhabitants'. In more forceful language, a Harrogate resident in 1899 could state: 'I have never heard any person condemn the presence of visitors coming to Harrogate. The only thing I have heard is complaints against excursionists who come by day trips, that they are not wanted, and they are not wanted now.' Having created the amenities of the spa, it was difficult to preserve its social exclusiveness.

The present character of Harrogate as a resort would seem strange to Victorian and Edwardian eyes. The spa is no longer the principal attraction, the 'Queen of Watering Places' has become 'Britain's Floral Resort'. The changes as they have affected the spa and its clientele will be discussed subsequently, as will the attempts that have been made to attract differing categories of visitor. It is sufficient to note now that 'visitor' and 'spa client' are no longer synonymous, but that residential visitors include as well holiday makers, conference delegates and businessmen.

With the cessation of the publication of visitors' lists during the First World War, objective analysis becomes more difficult. One reflection of change is the decline in the accommodation available in the resort. In 1939, Harrogate could accommodate 4702 visitors; by 1949, this figure had fallen to 3834 and it continued to fall to a total of 2969 in 1959. There has since been a slight recovery: the figure for 1961 was 3151. These are the official totals of the Publicity Department, and they suggest that approximately 500 may be added to cover rooms available at times of peak demand.

In considering the actual numbers of visitors, and their places of origin, evidence is available from a survey of 30 per cent of the hotels made by the writer in 1958, and from a questionnaire conducted by the Publicity Department in 1961, in which replies were received from twenty hotels. It is difficult to assess the number of holiday visitors in the town at the height of the season, but the maximum figure at any one time is probably considerably under 3000. The small hotels are well filled, but for several larger hotels August is a slack month and at times they may be no more than half full.

The distinction between the different types of hotels is increased when the period of stay is

13 The changing Resort

CHANGES in the type of visitor since 1918 have already been mentioned, with the decline in the socially significant Cure making a fundamental difference to the basis of the resort. Increasingly, visitors were attracted to Harrogate by the nature of the town itself, rather than by the medical facilities it could offer. The trend became evident between the wars, and Harrogate's publicity concentrated more and more on the attractions of the town as an inland resort, rather than on its facilities as a spa. Many 'special attractions' were promoted, and this approach has been pursued with increased vigour since 1945. Any list would be tedious, but such items as the national 'weeks' (French, Scottish and Italian weeks were held in 1962), the Halle Festival and the Spring Flower Show attract adherents.

The change in attitude is also seen in the improvements made by the Corporation in existing amenities. The value of the Valley Gardens was enhanced by improvements in layout in the 1930s, and more especially by the building of the extensive Sun Pavilion and Colonnade in 1933. Since 1945, floral displays have been increased in splendour and extent and earned Harrogate a justifiable reputation as 'Britain's Floral Resort'. An interesting parallel development was the acquisition at Harlow Car in 1949 of a 40-acre site for the trial gardens of the Northern Horticultural Society, a project undertaken with the active encouragement of the Corporation.

Nevertheless, the seasonal holiday trade alone is insufficient to be the mainstay of the resort, particularly so far as the larger luxury hotels are concerned. Business visitors are a useful increment, but far more hotels would have closed if Harrogate had not become an important centre for conferences. This trade began on a noticeable scale in the 1930s, and in 1937, thirty were held in Harrogate. After the war, it was revived, and with conscious municipal promotion, Harrogate became an important conference centre. By 1953, almost 150 conferences were being held each year. In 1961 the total was 170, with 44,490 delegates attending. The largest, and in many ways the most important, are the trade fairs, of which Harrogate now has an annual average of fifteen.

Harrogate has several advantages for the conference trade. It is easy of access from most parts of the country, it has several good hotels all within reach of the various conference halls, and it is in itself an attractive centre with excellent shops. It has, however, certain limitations, particularly the restriction placed on conference size by available hotel accommodation, and the size of halls. For conferences too big for a single hotel, the largest available hall is the Royal Hall, seating 1350, the same as the total number that can be accommodated in the principal hotels. The Lounge Hall, seating 750, and the Sun Pavilion, seating 700, are also used. One deficiency in facilities was remedied by the construction in 1959 of an Exhibition Hall adjacent to the Royal Hall, which enables many conferences having an exhibition as an integral part of their programme to be accommodated in Harrogate.

Conferences dovetail fairly well with the seasonal holiday trade. The peak demand falls in May and October, and there are none of major importance in July and August except those of an international character organized to coincide with the main holiday periods. They tend to benefit primarily the larger hotels, for most conferences naturally prefer to be accommodated in as few hotels as possible, though many smaller hotels do share in the business brought outside the principal holiday months by the larger conferences.

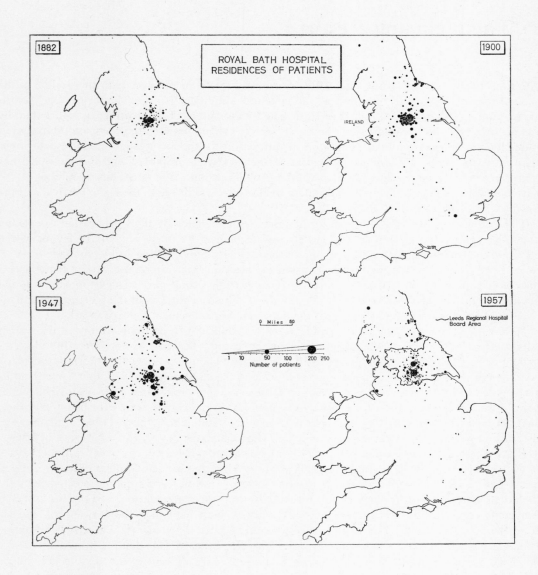

1882   ROYAL BATH HOSPITAL RESIDENCES OF PATIENTS   1900

IRELAND

1947   Leeds Regional Hospital Board Area   1957

0   Miles   50

1   10   50   100   200 250
Number of patients

14 The contemporary Spa

DESPITE the changed character of the resort, Harrogate as a spa is still very much alive. In the period between the wars, 'the Cure' maintained an uneasy popularity as the symbol of a social era which was gradually decaying. The years of the depression hit Harrogate particularly hard, but there was some revival of interest in the 1930s. In 1932 the Chancellor of the Exchequer and the Postmaster General were amongst those taking the Cure. In the 1920s, the totals of treatments given even surpassed those of the first decade of the century. In 1901, for example, there were 96,000 treatments given at the Royal Baths, and 120,207 in 1927. By 1936, however, the total had fallen to 72,665, with a recovery to 89,174 in 1938. Spa treatment had an increasingly scientific basis; the simple drinking of the waters declined rapidly from favour, and was no longer of much importance.

These changes were mirrored in the facilities provided. In 1930, the Victoria Baths were closed despite strenuous opposition, and treatments were concentrated at the Royal Baths. At the latter, extensions were planned in 1936, but were not complete until 1939. The Royal Pump Room over the Old Sulphur Well became an increasing anachronism. It was ultimately transformed into a museum in 1953, an eloquent reminder of the passing whims of fashion in the nature of spa treatment.

The Second World War accelerated changes which were already apparent. No matter what the inherent value of medical treatment at a spa, its prosperity depended on the existence of a social elite with the means to undergo a course of treatment whilst resident in the town. The social levelling of the inter-war years drastically reduced the numbers of those able to afford such a visit. By 1945, this process had been taken still further, and the outlook was bleak. In 1947, the number of treatments fell to 62,894. Revival came from an unexpected source, the creation of the National Health Service in 1948. Treatment was now available on prescription, and consequently within the reach of a far wider prospective clientele. Patients came in greatly increased numbers, until they exceeded the pre-war totals, and more than 150,000 treatments were given in a single year. The total for 1960-61 was 113,937. To the hotelier, the revival had a hollow ring. Even when patients are resident in the town, they normally come singly and seek the cheaper accommodation, as their period of stay is normally longer than that of the conference delegate or holiday visitor.

The area from which patients are drawn can be illustrated by mapping admissions to the Royal Bath Hospital. This Hospital, founded in 1825, has been dovetailed in administration with the Royal Baths since the creation of the National Health Service, and the total in-patient accommodation has expanded to 249 beds with the opening of the White Hart Hospital for ambulant patients. The pull of the spa for the more serious cases requiring in-patient treatment has always been markedly regional, but this trend has increased since 1948. Under the National Health Service, patients are normally sent to a spa within the area of the local Hospital Board if such a spa exists, and, if not, to the nearest one beyond the boundaries of the Board. In consequence the Royal Bath Hospital now draws by far the majority of its patients from places within the area covered by the Leeds and the Newcastle Regional Hospital Boards, the latter having no spa of its own.

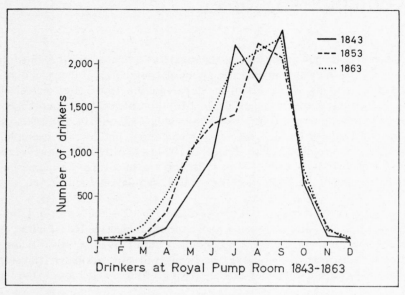

Drinkers at Royal Pump Room 1843-1863

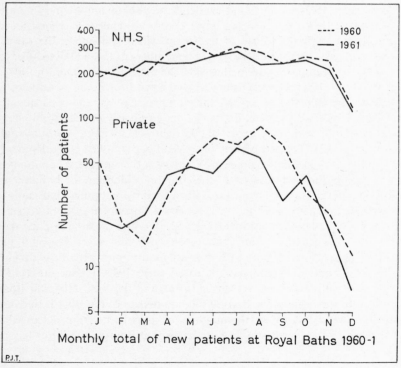

Monthly total of new patients at Royal Baths 1960-1

P.J.T.

15 The Season

THE season at the traditional spa was regulated not only by the weather, but also by the dictates of fashion. In the early nineteenth century, Harrogate's season extended from June to September, with a high season from the middle of August to the middle of September, 'between races at York and races at Doncaster', according to a diarist of 1816. The high season was marked by weekly balls at the principal hotels. Charles Greeves, the surveyor, wrote in his diary for 5 August 1842, 'the Granby Company attempted a Ball, but it was a total failure. Only 16 in the room'. The first ball a week later was described as 'very midling'. The last was held on 23 September, and for the 26th is the entry 'Granby music left'. In 1843, balls were held from 18 August, but not until the 25th was there sufficient company for it to be held in the dining-room. Granby company, however, was relatively exclusive, and there were marked social distinctions between different parts of the season. In 1839, Dr. Granville deliberately chose the end of July to visit Harrogate in order to see 'the tail of the "unwashed" and the head of the "exclusives" ', for 'visitors seem to rise in importance and in quantity of blood as the thermometer rises with the increasing heat of the summer sun'.

Later in the nineteenth century, the season was still fairly short, but with its peak in both August and September. Entries in the register of drinkers at the Royal Pump Room, plotted on the diagram, clearly show the pronounced nature of the peak. The fluctuations of actual numbers between July and September were often a reflection of the vagaries of the weather. There is little evidence of the average period of stay. Contemporary accounts suggest a fortnight or 3 weeks, but on the other hand, the subscription books of the Montpellier Pump Room, which have survived for 1862, show that despite a substantial reduction in tariff for periods of 2 weeks or more by far the majority of subscribers took tickets for a single week.

At the present day, any concept of a season is difficult to sustain. The differing types of visitors to Harrogate have already been discussed, and the implications of these differences on the duration of a season in the traditional sense are self-evident. The peak of the actual holiday season is relatively short, in July and August, but, particularly for the larger hotels, it is closely dovetailed with the spring and autumn peaks of the conference trade. The increase in coach traffic has increased the summer turnover of most of the larger hotels, and has led to difficulties in obtaining hotel accommodation for large conferences between June and mid-September. Even the winter months bring substantial trade: during the International Toy Fair, for example, held in January, more rooms are probably occupied in Harrogate than for any other single event.

The effective smoothing of peak demands has been shared by the Royal Baths, but for a very different reason. Patients treated under the aegis of the National Health Service can be summoned when required, and in consequence the Baths can be kept reasonably busy throughout the year and cater effectively for the increased number of patients. As the diagram shows, the remaining private patients (8.7 per cent of the total in 1960-61) are far more seasonal in their demands, an interesting reflection of earlier patterns. The graph is plotted on a logarithmic scale to emphasize monthly trends rather than absolute totals.

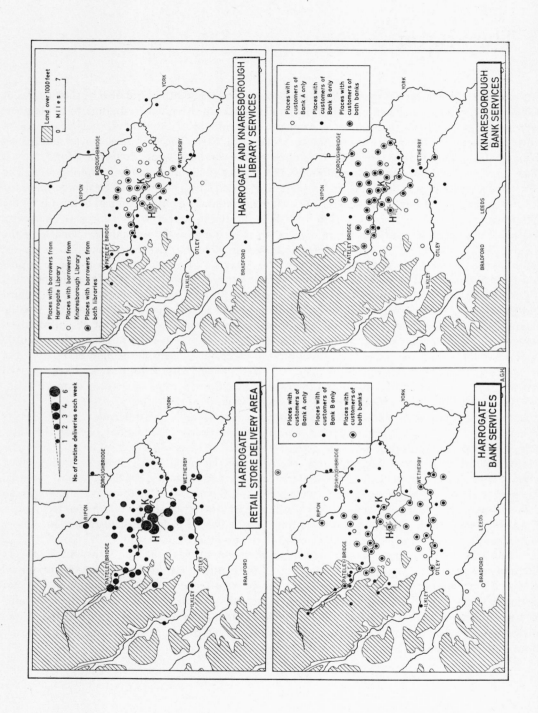

HARROGATE AND KNARESBOROUGH
LIBRARY SERVICES

- • Places with borrowers from Harrogate Library
- ○ Places with borrowers from Knaresborough Library
- ◉ Places with borrowers from both libraries

Land over 1000 feet

Miles
0   7

KNARESBOROUGH
BANK SERVICES

- ○ Places with customers of Bank A only
- • Places with customers of Bank B only
- ◉ Places with customers of both banks

HARROGATE
RETAIL STORE DELIVERY AREA

No. of routine deliveries each week
1   2   3   4   6

HARROGATE
BANK SERVICES

- ○ Places with customers of Bank A only
- • Places with customers of Bank B only
- ◉ Places with customers of both banks

BOROUGHBRIDGE
RIPON
PATELEY BRIDGE
YORK
WETHERBY
ILKLEY
OTLEY
BRADFORD
LEEDS

A.G.H.

40

16 Shopping and other Services

IMPORTANT though the hotels, the Baths, and the other elements of the resort are to the town, Harrogate is no longer solely a resort. In 1961, its population had reached 56,332, an increase of 11.6 per cent in ten years. Details of occupations are not yet available for the 1961 census, but in 1951, 41.9 per cent of the employed population were engaged in transport, commerce and personal service. If the administrative and professional groups are added to these, the total becomes 55.2 per cent. The picture emerges of a widely based servicing centre: 10.6 per cent were employed in retail trade alone.

Visitors, of course, contribute to the commerce of the town. Some businesses benefit more than others. Replies from sample cafés and restaurants to the Publicity Department's questionnaire in 1961 suggested that 65 per cent of their trade came from visitors, including 30 per cent from day visitors. A more varied selection of retail traders in the central shopping area attributed 37.8 per cent of their total custom to visitors, 19 per cent to day visitors alone.

The definition of visitor in this respect is obviously difficult, and day visitors include those attracted to the town by the excellence of its shopping facilities as much as by its qualities as a resort. Many of the specialist shops have a deservedly high reputation, and attract custom from a wide area. They are particularly concentrated in James Street, Parliament Street and Crescent Road, with outliers in Royal Parade and Montpellier Parade: the historical significance of this pattern has already been discussed.

Numerically, however, such shops are in a minority. It is interesting to see how much of the surrounding area looks to Harrogate for the provision of more basic shopping and other services. In this connection, the presence of Knaresborough is important, for despite its relatively small population, 9311 in 1961, it has retained its earlier commercial significance to a surprising degree. The maps are designed to illustrate the respective servicing areas of the two towns, by examining some carefully selected sample indices.

Few shops in Harrogate are of sufficient size to make regular deliveries over a wide area, but where such a service is given, it covers an area typical of many other services. In the example mapped, the Ure forms a fairly rigid northern limit. To the east the boundary is not so clearly defined, but is limited by the Nidd and the Ouse to a distance of about 10 miles. Southwards, the area extends into the valley of the Wharfe, and reaches from Otley to Wetherby. To the west, the area is limited by the Pennines, but extends as far up Nidderdale as Pateley Bridge. This area is almost exactly repeated by the map of bank services, particularly if the area served by both banks is considered. The only noticeable difference is to the north-east: the relative paucity of clients here is explained by the Knaresborough map. The area of overlap is again revealed by the map of library services.

The area served by Harrogate with basic services can therefore be fairly easily distinguished. It is not a large area for a town exceeding 55,000 in population, but these results take no account of Harrogate's more specialized shops and services or of the close proximity of competing centres such as Ripon, York, Otley and Leeds, and, to a lesser extent, Wetherby and Pateley Bridge. Most interesting is the continued importance of Knaresborough, serving a small but distinct area of its own. Only when Knaresborough cannot provide a particular service does Harrogate become an effective contributor in this area.

D
41

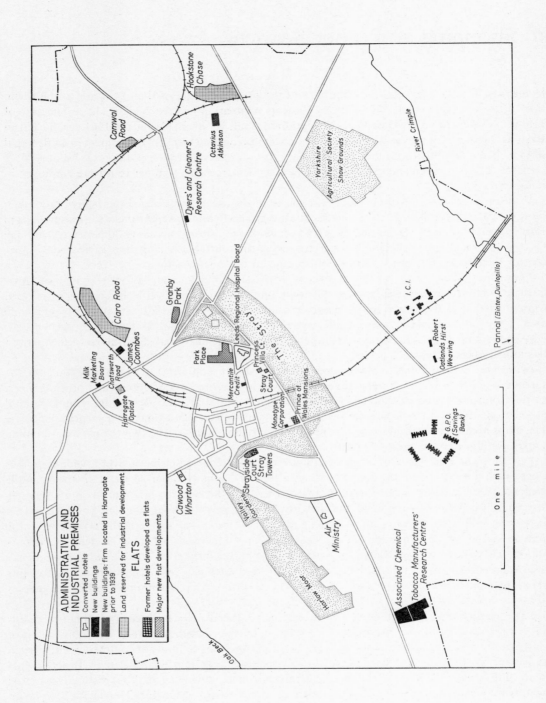

ADMINISTRATIVE AND
INDUSTRIAL PREMISES

Converted hotels

New buildings

New buildings: firm located in Harrogate
prior to 1939

Land reserved for industrial development

FLATS

Former hotels developed as flats

Major new flat developments

One mile

Hookstone Chase

Camwal Road

Octavius Atkinson

Dyers' and Cleaners'
Research Centre

Yorkshire
Agricultural Society
Show Grounds

River Crimple

Claro Road

Granby Park

Leeds Regional Hospital Board

The Stray

I.C.I.

Robert
Oatlands Hirst
Weaving

Pannal (Bintex, Dunlopillo)

Milk Marketing Board

Chatsworth Road

James Coombes

Harrogate
Optical

Park Place

Mercantile Credit

Princess
Villa Ct.

Stray
Court

Monotype
Corporation

Prince of
Wales Mansions

G.P.O.
(Savings Bank)

Cawood Wharton

Strayside Court

Stray Towers

Valley
Gardens

Air
Ministry

Harlow Moor

Associated Chemical

Tobacco Manufacturers'
Research Centre

Oak Beck

42

17 Administration and Industry

HARROGATE is a curious town, in that the social conditions which called it into being persisted so briefly, and left the resulting community to seek new bases for its continued existence. Part of its adaptation to changing circumstances has been seen in its post-war renaissance as a resort, but of even greater interest are the functions which Harrogate has only acquired recently, as they reflect more fundamental changes.

Paradoxically, the outbreak of war in 1939 brought the seeds of an eventual solution. In the wartime decentralization of Government departments away from London, the spas had a large part to play. They were all well away from the vulnerable south and east, and their hotels offered the prospect of adequate accommodation. The armed services made particular use of these facilities: Bath acquired departments of the Admiralty, Cheltenham of the War Office, and Harrogate of the Air Ministry. At the height of the war, 1800 were employed by the Air Ministry in Harrogate and almost all their work took place in requisitioned hotels. In addition, substantial numbers of G.P.O. employees were evacuated to the town and extensive hutted accommodation was built for their work on the south-western outskirts of the town.

After 1945, it became increasingly obvious that the vigorous survival of the town must depend on the acquisition of new functions as well as the exploitation of the old. The Air Ministry and the G.P.O. (Post Office Savings Bank) were still substantial employers: even today they employ about 750 and 1200 respectively. This success of Harrogate as an administrative centre pointed to one possible line of development. For manufacturing industry existing prospects were not so bright, nor did Harrogate wish to encourage any form of development harmful to the amenities of the town. The only two firms of more than local significance were both located on the outskirts. Octavius Atkinson & Sons Ltd., constructional engineers, had a site near the railway at Starbeck where today about 300 are employed. Bintex Ltd., manufacturers of latex foam and now a subsidiary of Dunlop, were sited adjacent to Pannal station, and today employ about 750.

Despite opposition, the Corporation rightly decided to encourage new developments, always provided they did not impair the amenities of the resort. Harrogate had several assets to offer. Of these perhaps the most important was the town itself, an extremely attractive residential centre with unusually good facilities for education. A close second was its position. It was only 15 miles north of Leeds, and within easy reach of other West Riding towns. It had adequate direct rail services with London, Liverpool and Scotland, and by a change at York or Leeds easy journeys could be made to most parts of the country. In the early post-war years, a not insignificant advantage was the number of derequisitioned but still empty hotels which could be converted into offices without the need for building licences.

From 1950, the effects of this Corporation policy have been gradually felt. Development may be arbitrarily grouped into three types, as each makes slightly different use of the town's facilities. In the first place there are those employers who took over empty hotels, and for whom the existence of such accommodation was the prime attraction following the wartime example of the Air Ministry. The former Southlands Hotel in Ripon Road became the administrative headquarters of a large civil engineering firm. The Leeds Regional Hospital Board has its headquarters in the Queen Hotel, moving there in 1951 after an abortive search for suitable premises in Leeds, Bradford and York.

Secondly there are those employers who recognized Harrogate's attractions as a centre, but who have built their own accommodation to suit their particular needs. Most such offices are naturally sited towards the periphery of the town, as for example the pleasant building in Skipton Road of the regional offices of the Milk Marketing Board, or the neat laboratories of the Dyers' and Cleaners' Research Organization in Knaresborough Road. A parallel development, though one more closely associated with the resort, was the establishing in 1951 of a permanent site south of Wetherby Road for the Yorkshire Agricultural Society's showground. Closely allied to this second group are the light industries which have moved into Harrogate. Again, their situation is peripheral, and the nature of such industry has been carefully controlled with the preservation of amenities in mind. The principal introduction has been the rainwear manufacturing business of Robert Hirst & Co. Ltd. The firm originally came to Harrogate in 1949, opening a small factory to help overcome the shortage of labour in Bradford, particularly acute so far as female labour was concerned. In this instance, Harrogate proved such a fruitful source of labour that the headquarters of the firm was moved here from Bradford, and some 300 are now employed.

Of all these post-war changes, one has been outstanding, and that has been the establishment in Harrogate of the administrative and research headquarters of the Fibres Division of Imperial Chemical Industries Limited.

I.C.I.'s need for these headquarters came to a head in 1952. Five years earlier I.C.I. had acquired the rights for the manufacture of 'Terylene' polyester fibre, a British discovery, and now, with the establishment of pilot plants and the commencement of work on the commercial plant at Wilton in north Yorkshire, it became desirable to set up a separate organization to take responsibility for the Company's interests in synthetic fibres manufacture.

In the choice of locality for the new headquarters, several requirements had to be borne in mind. The most important of these were ease of access to the plant at Wilton and to the major centres of the textile industry, proximity to a centre of textile technology, adequate facilities for education and recreation, and pleasant surroundings for work and residence. In addition, the site had to be sufficiently near a large town to ensure adequate supplies of labour, housing facilities and good train services.

These were formidable requirements, but the choice was soon narrowed down to the Leeds area. This had many advantages. There were adequate rail connections, whilst the whole of the textile area, and the three plants concerned with production, could be easily reached by car. The requirement for technical education were met by Leeds and Bradford. Leeds itself offered few attractive sites, but the area north of Leeds was scenically satisfying, and Harrogate a town large enough to supply the necessary services. York and Ilkley were among other possibilities.

The finding and acquisition of a site was not as easy as its theoretical location, and after an intensive search of the area, Crimple House, on the south side of Harrogate, was selected. With the whole-hearted approval of Harrogate Corporation, the 180 acres of the Crimple House estate were successfully acquired as the site for the new headquarters. Construction began in 1953, and by late 1955 all aspects of research, development and administration were accommodated here. I.C.I. now employs nearly 1300 people, approximately 5 per cent of the labour force in the town.

The major developments of the early 1950s successfully absorbed the post-war excess of labour in Harrogate. More recent arrivals have tended to be much smaller in scale, as typified by the Dyers' and Cleaners' Research Organization, the Tobacco Manufacturers' Standing Committee Research Centre and the more recent move to a site in Otley Road of the research department of the Associated Chemical Co. Ltd. The cumulative effect, however, is great, and the town has

Plate XI. The Changing Landscape: I

(*a*) Converted hotels: the former Queen Hotel, now the headquarters of the Leeds Regional Hospital Board.   *Photograph: Bertram Unné*

(*b*) Luxury flats: in the foreground, the former Stray Hotel, now, as Stray Towers, converted to flats. Beyond is Strayside Court, built new as flats.
Photograph: Bertram Unné

(*c*) New offices: Berkeley House, the headquarters of the Mercantile Credit Company Ltd.
Photograph: C. H. Wood

(*d*) New factories: the rainwear manufacturing premises of Robert Hirst & Co. Ltd.
Photograph: Graham Powell

Plate XII. The Changing Landscape: II

(*a*) Factory expansion: the premises of the Dunlo-pillo Division of Dunlop Rubber Co. Ltd. at Pannal.

(*b*) Research and administration: the headquarters of I.C.I. (Fibres Division).   *Photograph: I.C.I.*

(*c*) Multi-storey flats: an architect's drawing of the luxury flats being built on the Park Place site, 1962.
Photograph: Graham Powell

(*d*) Shopping area redevelopment: an architect's drawing of the shops and offices in Parliament Street projected in 1962 by London & Provincial Shop Centres Ltd.   *Photograph: S. W. Newbery*

effectively achieved diversification of function and employment. Even more important is the fact that this has been attained without losing anything of its character as a resort. Industrially, it cannot compare with Cheltenham and Leamington, but in its preservation of character as in continued medical importance it has outstripped other spas. A present-day Granville could still claim for it 'the very air of a watering place'.

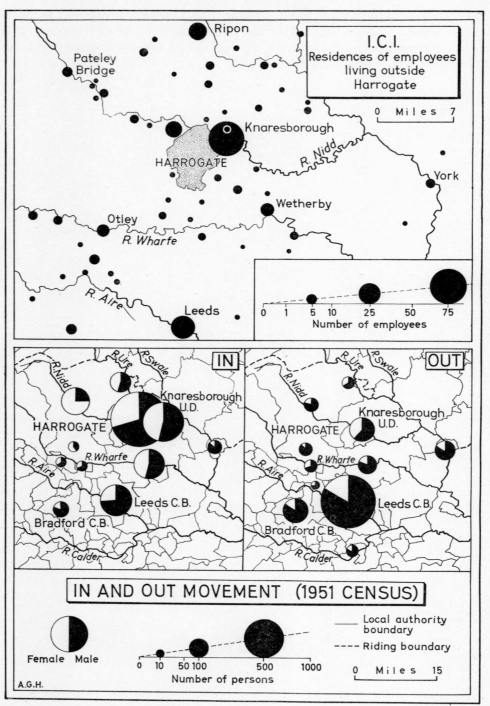

I.C.I.
Residences of employees
living outside
Harrogate

0 Miles 7

Ripon

Pateley
Bridge

Knaresborough

R. Nidd

HARROGATE

York

Wetherby

Otley

R. Wharfe

R. Aire

Leeds

Number of employees
0 1 5 10 25 50 75

IN

R.Ure R.Swale

R.Nidd

Knaresborough
U.D.

HARROGATE

R.Wharfe

R.Aire

Leeds C.B.

Bradford C.B.

R. Calder

OUT

R.Ure R.Swale

R.Nidd

Knaresborough
U.D.

HARROGATE

R.Wharfe

R.Aire

Leeds C.B.

Bradford C.B.

R. Calder

IN AND OUT MOVEMENT (1951 CENSUS)

Female Male

0 10 50 100 500 1000
Number of persons

Local authority
boundary

Riding boundary

0 Miles 15

A.G.H.

46

18 The movement of Labour

THE genesis in Victorian times of Harrogate's function as dormitory settlement has already been outlined. The Usual Residence and Place of Work tables of the 1951 census enable the extent of such movement to be analysed in some detail. There are limitations on their value, of which the most important is the restriction of entries to the larger areas of local government, no data being available, for example, for the component parishes of Rural Districts. Nevertheless, in the case of Harrogate, a clear picture emerges.

The total number entered in 1951 as living in Harrogate, but working outside the Borough was 2852: of these, only 18 per cent were females. Leeds stands out on the map of out-movement as by far the most important receiving centre, accounting in fact for 39 per cent of the total, whilst another 7.5 per cent went to Bradford. The majority of these are business men who have sought a more attractive residential town than the industrial West Riding affords. The existence of good communications facilitates this movement: in addition to journeys by car and bus, there are frequent and fast rail connections. As early as 1860, a local newspaper noted that the retention of an early morning train from Starbeck to Leeds during the winter months 'will have a tendency to increase the number of permanent residents in Harrogate'. The opening of the new station in 1862 made such commuting far easier. Harrogate's Victorian historian, W. Grainge, could write in 1871 that 'this gave a great impetus to the enlargement of the town, by bringing many merchants and manufacturers to reside here, whose places of business were in Leeds, Bradford and other large manufacturing towns of the West Riding'. It is not without significance that the rail link between Harrogate, Leeds and Bradford was the scene in 1954 of the first post-war scheme in Britain of modernization by the introduction of diesel railcar services: in this instance, the numbers travelling by train trebled in 3 months.

Harrogate is also in itself an attraction to labour. In 1951, in-movement exceeded out-movement in the census returns: 3514 people worked in Harrogate who were not resident there, or approximately 15 per cent of the total labour force. Of the total in-movement 35 per cent was female, a big contrast with the out-movement. Knaresborough contributed 30 per cent of the total, and the Nidderdale Rural District $16\frac{1}{2}$ per cent. The other major contributors were the Ripon and Pateley Bridge Rural District, 10 per cent, Leeds $9\frac{1}{2}$ per cent and Wetherby Rural District $7\frac{1}{2}$ per cent. Significantly, 53 per cent of those moving from the Ripon and Pateley Bridge area were females, but only 26 per cent of those from Leeds.

A more detailed picture of this movement can be obtained by mapping the homes of employees of individual firms, and this has been possible in the case of I.C.I., whose influence, of course, was not apparent in the 1951 data. There are two elements in this movement, although it is not possible to separate them in practice. There are those employees who reside outside Harrogate either from choice, or through lack of suitable housing in the town, and there are those belonging to the adjacent small towns and rural areas who have sought work in Harrogate through lack of local opportunities or the desire for better prospects. Of the total employed, more than 76 per cent live in Harrogate itself, and $5\frac{1}{2}$ per cent in Knaresborough. It is immediately noticeable that the area from which labour is drawn corresponds very closely to the area over which Harrogate provides basic services. The only anomaly is the extension into Airedale, a reflection of I.C.I.'s link with the textile manufacturing of the West Riding.

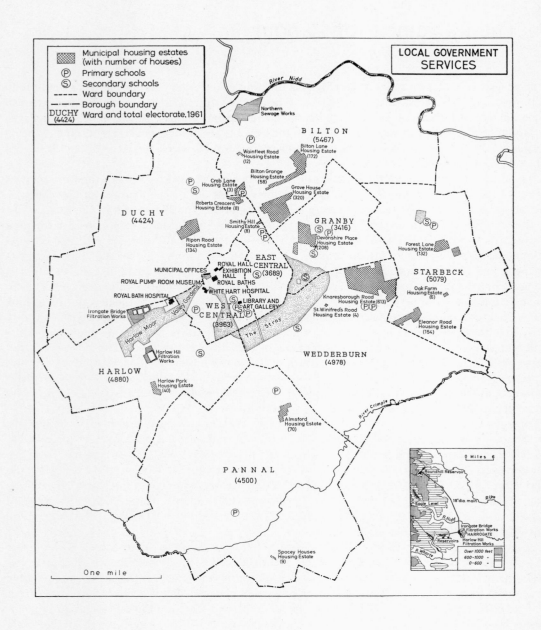

LOCAL GOVERNMENT
SERVICES

Municipal housing estates
(with number of houses)
(P) Primary schools
(S) Secondary schools
- - - - Ward boundary
-·-·- Borough boundary
DUCHY Ward and total electorate,1961
(4424)

River Nidd

Northern
Sewage Works

BILTON
(5467)

Wainfleet Road
Housing Estate
(12)

Bilton Lane
Housing Estate
(172)

Bilton Grange
Housing Estate
(58)

Crab Lane
Housing Estate
(3)

Grove House
Housing Estate
(320)

Roberts Crescent
Housing Estate (8)

DUCHY
(4424)

Smithy Hill
Housing Estate
(8)

GRANBY
(3416)

Ripon Road
Housing Estate
(134)

Devonshire Place
Housing Estate
(208)

Forest Lane
Housing Estate
(132)

EAST
CENTRAL
(3689)

STARBECK
(5079)

MUNICIPAL OFFICES
ROYAL HALL
EXHIBITION
HALL
ROYAL PUMP ROOM MUSEUM
ROYAL BATHS
WHITE HART HOSPITAL
ROYAL BATH HOSPITAL
LIBRARY AND
ART GALLERY
WEST
CENTRAL
(3963)

Oak Farm
Housing Estate
(6)

Irongate Bridge
Filtration Works

Knaresborough Road
Housing Estate (613)

St.Winifred's Road
Housing Estate (4)

Eleanor Road
Housing Estate
(154)

Valley Gardens

The Stray

Harlow Moor

Harlow Hill
Filtration
Works

WEDDERBURN
(4978)

HARLOW
(4880)

Harlow Park
Housing Estate
(40)

Almsford
Housing Estate
(70)

River Crimple

PANNAL
(4500)

Spacey Houses
Housing Estate
(9)

One mile

0 Miles 6

Roundhill Reservoir

Eagle Level
18"dia. main

R.Ure

R.Nidd

Irongate Bridge
Filtration Works
HARROGATE
Harlow Hill
Filtration Works

Reservoirs

R.Whafe

Over 1000 feet
600-1000
0-600

48

19 Municipal Services and Local Government

IT is fitting that the concluding map should be concerned with aspects of municipal services and local government. Throughout this account, the influence of local administration has been implicit. Sir William Holford aptly remarked in 1955 that 'the individual spa town does not stand so much in need of planning as of enterprise, a watchful eye to anticipate changes, and the necessary capital to meet this in a highly competitive industry'. Harrogate has had such enterprise in full measure. It is beyond the scope of this work, concerned as it is with the evolution of the function and the form of the town, to attempt a history of its local government and to recall the personalities involved. That task has, in any case, been most efficiently performed by H. H. Walker, whose book *Harrogate's Past*, was published in 1959 to mark the seventy-fifth anniversary of the incorporation of the Borough. Nevertheless, Harrogate's particular fortune in this respect must be recalled. Its prosperity as a spa, however short-lived, and its necessary adaptation of function after 1918, both owe their success in no small measure to the vigour and foresight of its Council and officers. Many aspects of this have already been discussed — the development of the municipally owned spa area, with unrivalled facilities, the preservation and beautification of the public open spaces of the Stray and the Valley Gardens, and the active encouragement of new administrative and industrial enterprises since 1945. Few towns indeed owe more of their present nature to their local government.

More routine aspects of local government must not be forgotten, and one which deserves some attention is the provision of water supplies. Prior to the 1840s, supplies had come entirely from springs and wells, such as the Cold Well in Cold Bath Road, 'a fine cleare and sweete Spring of Comon water very good to wash eyes and pleasant to drinke' as Celia Fiennes described it in 1697. With the growth of the spa to a town, such provision rapidly became inadequate, and a private company was established in 1846 to provide increased supplies. Reservoirs were built on Harlow Moor and near Cornwall Road, and, after 1858, on land in Haverah Park, where four were eventually sited — Ten Acres, capacity 30 million gallons, in 1869, Beaver Dyke East, 118.5 million gallons and Beaver Dyke West, 28.5 million gallons, in 1888, and Scargill, 192.1 million gallons, in 1896. The undertaking was purchased by the Corporation in 1898, who then began to look for additional reservoir sites to augment capacity. The Oak Beck system was by now fully utilized, and the catchment area of the upper Nidd was being exploited by Bradford. The nearest alternative was on a tributary of the Ure, and Roundhill reservoir was completed in 1912. This has a catchment area of 3000 acres, and a capacity of 525 million gallons. It was then estimated that Harrogate's total supplies were adequate for a town of 80,000 inhabitants, so remarkable foresight was shown at a time when its population was less than 35,000. The undertaking is now merged in the Claro Water Board, but remains a tribute to Harrogate's municipal enterprise. The increasing *per capita* demands for water, as well as the growth of the town, have brought the need for further supplementation of supplies; this is being met by the Eagle Level scheme on which work began in April 1962. This utilizes a spring near Pateley Bridge, first tapped by lead workings more than a century ago but not previously exploited. It has a daily output of 1.7 million gallons, part of which is now distributed in the Ripon and Pateley Bridge area and in 200,000 gallons a day compensation to the River Nidd: the remainder will flow through a new main more than 13 miles long to Harrogate.

GENERAL STATISTICS, 1961

Area of Borough in acres	8,320	Rateable Hereditaments	
Population	56,332	Domestic	18,393
Road mileage	114·08	Commercial	2,806
Rateable Value	£899,837	Industrial	75
Product of penny rate	£3,645	Others	380

FINANCE

COST OF SERVICES AS A PROPORTION OF EACH £1 OF RATE PAID, 1960-61

BOROUGH SERVICES

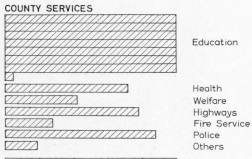

Highways and Lighting
Health: Parks, Refuse, Sewage
Library, Art Gallery and Museum
Entertainments and Publicity
General Administration
Others
Surpluses

COUNTY SERVICES

Education

Health
Welfare
Highways
Fire Service
Police
Others

0   1   2   3   4   5 shillings

For each £1 of rate paid   £1 17s. 10·3d. is contributed by the Central Government

HOUSING

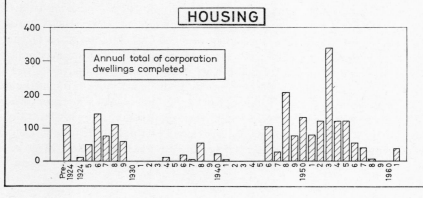

Annual total of corporation dwellings completed

50

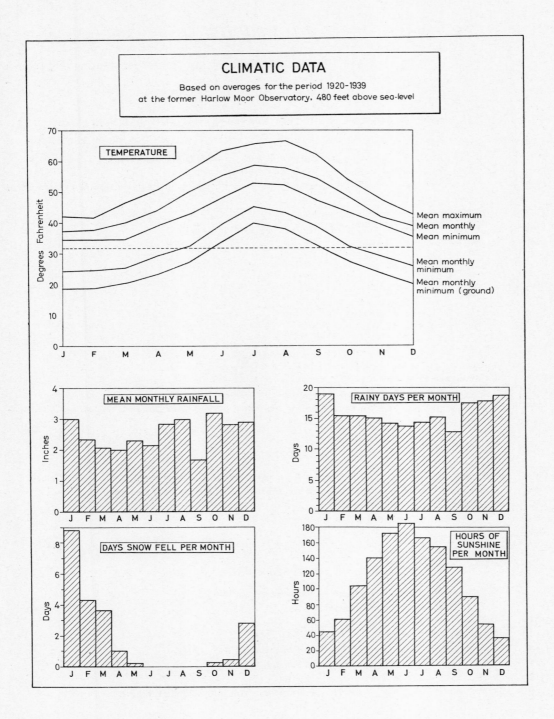

CLIMATIC DATA

Based on averages for the period 1920-1939
at the former Harlow Moor Observatory, 480 feet above sea-level

TEMPERATURE

Degrees Fahrenheit

Mean maximum
Mean monthly
Mean minimum
Mean monthly minimum
Mean monthly minimum (ground)

J F M A M J J A S O N D

MEAN MONTHLY RAINFALL

Inches

J F M A M J J A S O N D

RAINY DAYS PER MONTH

Days

J F M A M J J A S O N D

DAYS SNOW FELL PER MONTH

Days

J F M A M J J A S O N D

HOURS OF SUNSHINE PER MONTH

Hours

J F M A M J J A S O N D

51

Bibliography

This list is far from comprehensive, but will give guidance to any reader wanting to pursue a particular point further.

GENERAL WORKS ON BRITISH SPAS AND INLAND RESORTS

1734-40   T. SHORT, *History of Mineral Waters* (2 vols.).

1841   A. B. GRANVILLE, *The Spas of England, and Principal Sea-Bathing Places* (3 vols.).

1919   T. D. LUKE, *Spas and Health Resorts of the British Isles.*

1939   E. W. GILBERT, 'The growth of inland and seaside health resorts in England', *Scottish Geographical Magazine*, vol. 105.

1947   J. A. R. PIMLOTT, *The Englishman's Holiday.*

1951   British Medical Association, *The Spa in Medical Practice.*

1951   W. ADDISON, *English Spas.*

MEDICAL

1626   E. DEANE, *Spadacrene Anglica.*

1652   J. FRENCH, *The Yorkshire Spaw.*

1792   T. GARNETT, *Treatise on the Mineral Waters of Harrogate.*

GEOLOGICAL

1908   C. FOX-STRANGWAYS, *The Geology of the Country North and East of Harrogate.*

1924   P. F. KENDALL and H. E. WROOT, *The Geology of Yorkshire.*

1938   R. G. S. HUDSON and others, 'The geology of the country around Harrogate', *The Proceedings of the Geologists' Association*, vol. 49.

HISTORICAL

1798   E. HARGROVE, *The History of the Castle, Town and Forest of Knaresborough.*

1871   W. GRAINGE, *The History and Topography of Harrogate and the Forest of Knaresborough.*

1922   W. J. KAYE, *Records of Harrogate.*

1954   W. HAYTHORNTHWAITE, *Harrogate Story.*

1959   H. H. WALKER, *Harrogate's Past.*

TOPOGRAPHICAL

The dates quoted initially are those to which the description applies.

1626   M. STANHOPE, *Newes out of York-shire.*

1632   M. STANHOPE, *Cures without Care.*

1697   C. MORRIS (ed.) *The Journeys of Celia Fiennes*, 1947.

1756   E. A. BAKER (ed.) *The Life and Opinions of John Buncle, Esq.*, 1904.

1771   T. SMOLLETT, *The Expedition of Humphry Clinker*, 1785.

1812   B. HOFLAND, *A Season at Harrogate.*

1816   D. W. SMITH, *Diary of a Visit to Harrogate.* (Manuscript in the Public Library).

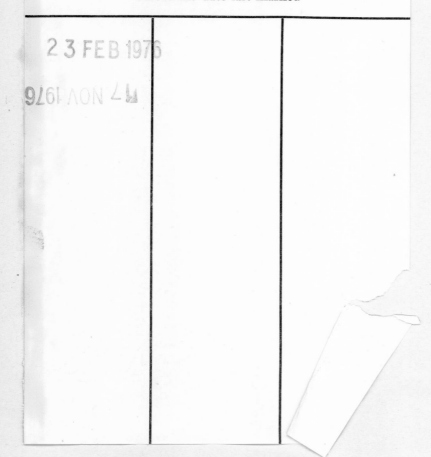

Keep 8/2000 LD

CHRIST CHURCH COLLEGE
CANTERBURY

This book must be returned (or renewed) on or
before the date last marked